The Fairy Queen

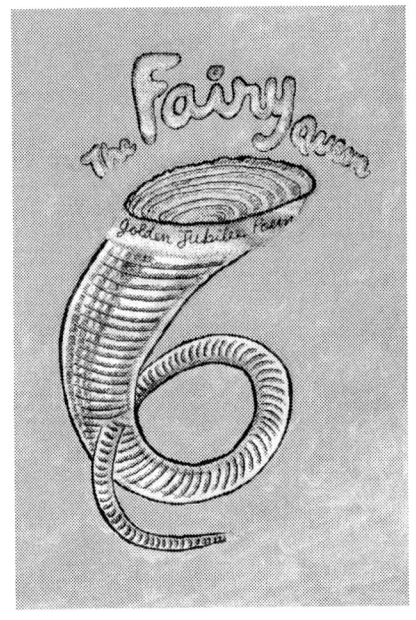

This is the first edition, September 2002
Published by justWords limited,
9 Queens Road, Keynsham, Bristol,
BS31 2NE, Great Britain
http://www.justwords.demon.co.uk
orderline: athais@justwords.demon.co.uk

ISBN 1-901382-01-X
Copyright © justWords Limited

Designed, produced & managed by AThaiS Limited

Bureau services and advice: The Skriptorium,
6 Lower Park Row, Clifton, Bristol BS1 5BJ UK

Printed & bound in Great Britain by MWL Digital Solutions Ltd,
Unit 13, Pontyfelin Industrial Estate, New Inn, Pontypool, NP4 0DQ

The moral rights of the author, Thomas Albert Fox,
have been asserted in accordance with the
Copyright, Designs and Patents Act 1988.

All rights reserved. No part of this publication may be reproduced, stored in a retrieval system, or transmitted, in any form or by any means, electronic, mechanical, photocopying, recording or otherwise, without prior permission of the publisher.

justWords is a new diasporas publisher

Cover illustration by Siriluck Kedseemake
ภาพหน้าปกวาดโดย สิริลักษณ์ เกตุศรีเมฆ [1]
From an idea by Thomas Albert Fox

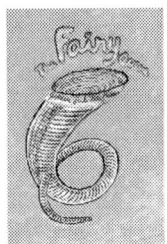

The Fairy Queen is certified a GM[2] free publication.

---

[1] Translation of line above into Thai
[2] GM free: "Government Money" free, that is free of committees, councils and the concomitant general crud of special initiatives, lottery funds and other funny money, including corporate sponsors. Independently certified by B F Garret & Co.

Thomas Albert Fox

"The Fairy Queen"

Edited by Terry Edwards

justWords

http://www.justwords.demon.co.uk

Contents

	Page
Acknowledgements	i
The Fairy Queen	1
Introduction to the poem	5
Commentary stanza by stanza	60
Conclusion	88

Acknowledgements

After many years as Thomas Albert Fox's unpaid editor, I have finally persuaded him to release this single poem for publication. Of the seven volumes of works in progress his intention, and mine, is to publish each volume as a complete work[3]. To date this has resulted in perpetual deferment as there seems always "another" poem to be included that will be "available soon" and which is essential to the overall "philosophy" of this or that particular volume. Thus, publishing this 'odd' poem, "The Fairy Queen", with my critical apparatus, is very much a way of avoiding the constraints of "The Plan" Fox has in mind for his work as a whole.

Obviously, publishing work of this kind can only lose money, unless contaminated by GM^2 (which it is not), so there is no economic incentive to force the pace of publication. In any case, it is in some regards my own efforts as editor to produce some sort of critical apparatus to go with Fox's work that is also a delaying factor. In this regard, I have to admit that the next volume for publication, "Songs of Nocence", has in fact been delayed for this very reason as the forty one songs involved are completed.

As to Fox himself, suffice it to say that his pathological reclusiveness is as if he has fallen permanently among monsters over the edge of an earth that has turned out to be flat after all. He has led a life that has made him a stranger in his own mind.

---

[3] Details of each volume are published on
http://www.justwords.demon.co.uk , but in summary they are:
Volume one,	"English Wounds".
Volume two,	"Inscriptions".
Volume three,	"Insistence".
Volume four,	"Intercourse".
Volume five,	"Presence".
Volume six,	"Songs of Nocence".
Volume seven,	"The Charred Lord".

In regard to the considerable reference to the Elizabethan poet Edmund Spenser throughout, both Fox and I are truly grateful for the extraordinary effort of Richard Bear's scholarly on-line "Renascence Editions". Bear is credited by his legatee, the Faculty of English, University of Cambridge[4], with the creation of the earliest on-line Renaissance English literary texts. Certainly, for both of us this kind of visionary effort, and Cambridge's excellent back-up, is what makes the internet truly worthwhile in spite of its many failings, indeed makes its freedom worth protecting from those who feel they should 'take care' of it, in the interests of 'protecting' we the public, of course.

In fact, the edition of Spenser I have quoted from, is a very tattered, ISBNless, 19th century print published by Routledge without a date. It seems complete with all its pages, though some are now loose. When in doubt I have consulted Bear's "Renascent Editions" online and enjoyed pottering about the site in general.

To us, Richard Bear and his ilk are all heroes! As mere unscholarly individuals sharing a few PCs and a couple of telephone lines, neither Fox nor I have passes into the institutionalised resources available in the libraries and databanks of the great universities and other multi-national corporations, nor have we the time to spend in them if we did. In any case,

> "... The library defends itself, immeasurable as the truth it houses, deceitful as the falsehood it preserves. A spiritual labyrinth, it is also a terrestrial labyrinth. You might enter and you might not emerge. And having said this, I would like you to conform to the rules of the abbey."[5]

---

[4] A superb public interest site, free of charges, excellent: http://www.english.cam.ac.uk/spenser/welcome.htm
[5] Umberto Eco, "The Name of the Rose", Secker & Warburg, 1983, page 38.

Thus, we have virtually avoided the dangers of the terrestrial labyrinth and its rules, if not the spiritual. So, Bear's creation of convenient, genuine public online access to such great stuff is very much to be encouraged.

Our instinct is that Edmund Spenser would have been a natural on-liner; just imagine the author of "The Faerie Queene" substituting mere quill and ink for the massive resources of the internet, his wordprocessor at the ready. The mind boggles! Perhaps, we should take on board Michael Rogers' concern, even in 1990, about 'intelligent' idea processors providing so called value-added even to wordprocessors, or the eruption of "logorrhea" from on-screen editing, &/or the "mushing" of intellectual structure through ease of re-arranging paragraphs. However, we may be heartened by his conclusion that,

> —but new writing technology, by elevating the common denominator, will allow the inspiration to rise from higher ground than language today inhabits.[6]

It is in this regard that Fox and I imagine the awesome Spenser grasping his chances with the wordprocessor and the World Wide Web.

I am grateful to Thomas Albert Fox for his coinage of the term "cybennial". In short he has combined 'cyber', 'cycle' and 'millennial' to make 'cybennial' as a convenient term for the present post-postmodern new era. This is more fully explained in the introduction.

I am also grateful to Lawrence James Attree for reading the early online draft of the critical apparatus and for his helpful comments and suggestions, kind encouragement and gentle forbearance.

Terry Edwards, June 2002, at Keynsham, Somerset, UK

---

[6] Michael Rogers, "Computers and Language", in "The State of the Language", page 299, edited by Christopher Ricks and Leonard Michaels, UCP USA, Faber and Faber UK, 1990.

The Fairy Queen

On the Occasion of Seeing Her Majesty
Queen Elizabeth II Process at Bath
During Her Golden Jubilee[7] Tour
the Second Day of May AD 2002.

---

[7] Jubilee is given by Ayto, Chambers & ODCC to refer to Jewish Law (Leviticus 25), 'a year occurring once every fifty years when Jewish slaves regained their freedom, and land reverted to its former owners'; the Hebrew *yōbhēl* meant 'ram' or 'ram's horn' from which a peal was blown to announce a special year. Thus, 'Jubilee' means literally 'year of the Ram's horn', this later became embroiled with the separate L. etymological root *jūbilare* which meant 'to call out' or 'to shout for joy'. It is therefore a word involving an Old Testament Jewish rite in which the fanfare was a central behaviour, with a shouting out. The somewhat genteel and much reserved City of London Jubilee Reception for the Queen, luncheon 31st May 2002, is, like so many apparently Victorian traditions, much rooted in the primitive past, and in fact the event is fundamentally punctuated by fanfares and shouts.

By the way, throughout I have used the following abbreviated titles:
* Ayto = "Dictionary of Word Origins", John Ayto, 1990, Columbia Marketing, 1994.
* Brewer's = Brewer's Dictionary of Names", Edited Adrian Room, Cassell, 1992.
* Chambers = "Chambers Dictionary of Etymology", Edited Robert K Barnhart, 1988.
* ODCC = Oxford Dictionary of the Christian Church", Edited F L Cross, OUP, 1963.
* OE = Old English which includes AS Anglo-Saxon.
* Pollington = "Wordcraft Wordhoard and Wordlists: Concise New English to Old English Dictionary and Thesaurus", Stephen Pollington, Anglo-Saxon Books, 1993.
* Skeat = "The Concise Dictionary of English Etymology", Walter W Skeat (1835-1912), Wordsworth Editions, 1993.
* SOED = "Shorter Oxford English Dictionary On Historical Principles", C T Onions' third edition, Oxford, 1959.

1
We had waited long and hard for this
To peer through the crowd to see her for real
It was something we simply couldn't miss
And there I was lost in the forest of faces
Fenced by the rails of galvanised steel
Where we had pressed to keep our places
When of a sudden she was here
A person you could almost feel
So close she seemed and clear.

2
There was such a flurry as she passed us by
Lost in a crowd of her own
But in a trice the Duke was nigh
To talk and shake then haul away
The man so firm behind her throne
Though sailing free and easy in his day
When he could say just what he thought
Till in great shoals his words were blown
Fraught by groans the fleet had caught.

3
His netted words had flashed upon the air
Until they landed lolling on the beach
To twist and lie then rot into the daily fare
Where he'd floundered high and dry
His thoughts all wracked with speech
For when pressed hard he wasn't shy
And never took the time to hide
But waded in the open breach
To stand against the running tide.

4
But now a changing troublesome sea
With old Britannia turned to scrap
Froths and foams the mother of the free
To swamp her shores with soapy waves
That wash old fabrics with pure crap
Until she craves and swells and raves
And stings with tears the public sighs
As all her English turns to rap
While soap gets in her eyes.

5
And in her wounds those salty smears
Take solace in her pain
And work their way into the fears
That worm apart the common ground
To open up the hidden bane
Wherein her roots are found
Among the splits in stem and stock
Beneath the fields of fearful slain
And bloody heads she wrested on her block.

6
But here beneath the ancient oaks
We cut the sacred mistletoe
To hang its green on party jokes
Converting christmas to our needs
While all the groves we used to know
Are now the graves of buried seeds
That grow and burst from time to time
So blood again can quickly flow
To hunt our hearts with secret crime.

7
And as our eyes drink in this scene
Our lips are moved our tongues unfold
To find the fairy Queen
Here among our hearts of oak
Where we had stayed all frozen cold
Until she heard us cry and woke
And raised her self again on high
Her head all bowed with gold
That glistered through the broken sky.

8
When people saw that living light
And felt the goodness shining down
They knew their wait through the long cold night
Had proved worthwhile at last
And as it rose all blinding bright it cast its brilliance down
An eye of light all tangled in the past
For here beneath the canopy upon the crowded floor
Right before their very eyes shines the golden crown
And all must bow to find the path toward the ancient lore.

9
Thus winding through the endless wood
The people with the crown still walk their well worn way
Their heads bowed down to find the good
Laid fallen here among these tangled roots
That delve the common clay
To feed the new and growing shoots
That raise themselves and break the mould
To seek the light of day
Where a vision holds them fast as in those days of old.

Introduction

As Fox's editor I felt it would be helpful to begin to open up his Golden Jubilee Poem "The Fairy Queen" with a few ideas. Though my intention is modest, there is the danger that some may prefer, or give precedence to the notes over the poem itself. This would be to fall into the error of the parcel[8] as my object is merely to show that his "Fairy Queen" is rooted in the collective British psyche, that it draws from a well of meaning sunk deep in the minds of ordinary people; and not merely the 'ethnically' British (Britons, Celts, Latins, Angles, Saxons and Vikings alike[9]), but of all people of the earth no matter the particular guise their cultures have taken on. It seems to Fox that there is a common source in the nature of humankind whereof there is an ineradicable instinct to personify a *wellhead* whereof natural thirsts for protection and consideration may be slaked, a supping

---

[8] The 'error of the parcel' is best understood in terms of the children's party game 'pass the parcel'. In this you pass the poem from one thought to the next, with each thought frantically unwrapping the covers of meaning, yet never reaching that sweet and joyous revelation beneath a last layer where lies the real present itself; here is merely a feeling toward the strain of uncontinuing music, a tense stretching toward nothing, the unending of the game.

[9] Of course, one might take the Venerable Bede's analysis of "The Situation of Britain and Ireland, And of Their Ancient Inhabitants" (Chapter I) as a rather salutary starting point. He lists the five nations who follow the five books of the divine law of which the Latin tongue is by the study of the Scriptures common amongst them: the English, Britons, Scots, Picts and Latins. This chapter in Bede should be compulsory reading for the leaders of the various petty nationalist parties of the now nine countries comprising the 'United Kingdom (England, Monarchless Ireland, Monarchist Ireland, Scotland, Wales, Cornwall, Manxland, Channel Islands, and the ninth country: Great Britain).

in common from that mythic chalice, that cauldron containing and pertaining the common blood of an humankind now buried in our collective past. Though "history is bunk", 'the past' is inevitably collective, if it exists at all.

All this may suggest that to know the poem you need to know these details about some of the ideas at the roots of Fox's enchanted or enchanting, "Fairy[10] Queen". Not at all; but poetry is on the side of ideas, or the ideas within which we shelter, and Fox is a poet. My intention is merely to save you time, not to explain "The Fairy Queen", not to neuter your own independent scrutiny. Or pitch you against the paradox of destruction by deconstruction, to find unsurprisingly that the parts are indeed less than the whole.

In any case, "The Fairy Queen" has given me the opportunity to illustrate something of the complexity and intensity of thought and feeling involved in Fox's poetry generally; though, let me hasten to make clear, the particular Spenserian character of the poetic machinery here will not be found in Fox's work generally, but complexity and intensity does extend throughout, no matter how

---

[10] Like Edmund Spenser, the great 16th century Elizabethan poet, Fox weaves the etymological threads of "Fairy" to create a substantial, meaningful shape for cybennial senses to grope, to clasp and to raise, and to sup that which intoxicates the imagination. Through Chambers and Skeat and Brewer's and Ayto and Pollington and SOED we have 'fairy' through 'fay' as *fate*, as that which is *spoken*, as enchanting, as *cant*, as whining song, as *canto* in Christian church, as *bannen* to proclaim, as stop, prevent, exile by proclamation, etc etc; and with all the modern and cybennial connotations we find that Britain of 2002 AD is "Faerie" which means a land of fairies, an insubstantial land wherein all is media magic and the web is spun to deceive, a virtual never-never land. Is nothing new? Yes, see the commentary below on Stanza 7, when the "fairy" embraces not only all these enchantments but also the 'enchantment' of homosexuality.

simple a poem may appear. In this regard, complexity is intensity in Fox's work.

There is perhaps a need to touch on the very form of these notes as they are tacked to the poem. They are designed in the context of being electronically read rather than being read on paper in the conventional book or journal form of a material block of hard printing. Thus, the inconvenience of shuffling to and from each note as the need arises is quite eschewed. To read this on screen, as a file, you would have the facility of the yellow square popping up[11] with the note when the cursor is placed over the note number[12]. This makes it quick and convenient to have a look at what it's on about, and then to go to it for the accurate view[13].

---

[11] Yellow square.

[12] Note 12.

[13] When reading on screen, the yellow 'pop-up' may not fully format as per the note itself. For example, quotations within the note do not show in their same format. This slight glitching of the formatting across applications sometimes affects layouts as they transfer from say Microsoft Word through to Quark or other typesetting application and through to, say, Microsoft Frontpage and thence to the internet through ISP/FTP onto the World Wide Web. Thus, certain minor glitches may make it necessary to re-enter this piece of work by re-keying the whole thing character by character, which is not possible in terms of the time and resources I have available as Fox's editor; nor is it intrinsically worthwhile. Thus, the full use of cybennial hypertextuality may not quite come-off in one seamless (ie economical) process. Nevertheless, I have set up this piece, as with all the justWords works, so that it is available in cybennial form, if sometimes slightly glitched across applications. This cybennial approach in effect creates a new syntax wherein the notes become all of a piece with the work, ceasing to appear as awkward appendages simply for technical matter that would disrupt the run of the main text. This is to form part of the new grammar (as etiquette) of English which would also embrace hypertextual material.

If you read this on the internet, online, then you should generally have the hypertexting facility available which amounts to the same degree of convenience, as it were to parallel read both the main text and the notes as you go. This partly involves the developing 'new syntax'[14] of instant vertical movement using the electronically tagged note or reference and the hypertexting horizontal capability of material produced for the World Wide Web[15]. This allows me to provide notes that give information that is often, though not always, widely available at the convenience of the reader. It saves the reader time in having to go elsewhere to look up stuff that could be a help in getting close to the poem. I take Ricks' dictum to heart here,

> Sometimes a particular reader may not need the particular information, [given in a note] but then — as William Empson said — 'it does not require much fortitude to endure seeing what you already know in a note'.[16]

Of course, he and Empson were talking about information and not explanation, so I may have erred here and there, even to have strayed into the Empsonian conundrum that,

> In a sense it [poetic meaning] cannot be explained in language, because to a person who does not understand it any statement of it is as difficult as the original one, while to a person who does

---

[14] fox has coined this the "syntrax and orthology" of cybennial english, or pure 'textuation'.

[15] The hypertexted version of Fox's "Queen" can be found on the justWords website http://www.justwords.demon.co.uk

[16] Edited by Christopher Ricks, "T. S. Eliot: Inventions of the March Hare, Poems 1909-1917", Faber and Faber, 1996, page xxvi.

understand it a statement of it has no meaning because no purpose.[17]

However, the distinction between providing pure information, unspun as it were, is more likely to be a virtuous aspiration than an actual achievement.

The book form of this work has had to be reshaped by converting the mass of references and notes from endnotes to footnotes at the base of each page because they are best read as you go along. In this respect the book form is less convenient than any of the electronic forms. Nevertheless, it has the advantages of materiality and limit, and once printed cannot be altered and 'improved', as is the case with electronic forms[18]. In book form Fox's work, including the original cover painting, will normally be treated as definitive objects limited in number and individualised with dated signatures and personalised dedications.

Thus, each object (incidentally containing that particular edition of the text) is unique in itself, an actual carnal (material) 'Bitzanesque'[19] object. An

---

[17] William Empson, "Seven Types of Ambiguity", Pelican, 1973 (1930), page 22.

[18] There is also the key point that a conventionally printed book needs only an human intermediary to be revealed, whereas electronic texts in their archival forms are highly susceptible to very rapid obfuscation, and then complete loss because of technological 'improvements', the irrepressible and expensive hard and soft upgrading. Thus, as time passes, the electronic forms of this book will need the mediation of ever more sophisticated technical support and investment to enable continuing human accessibility.

[19] Ion Bitzan, Romanian artist 1924-96, although freed from political constraint with the fall of Nicolæ Ceaucescu, Christmas 1989, most of his work was done in a country subject to the repressive, concentration camp like controls of the Securitate, the Romanian secret police. An important aspect of Bitzan's work is his treatment of the book as object. He makes his art express the nature of books as things-in-themselves among us. Of course, such individuation is not

actual rather than a virtual object, not a cyberspatial phantom, but phenomenal object, "a real mirage"[20]. Each such carnal object will need to be sold at a premium. The premium will serve to support Fox's work with the object of funding the costs involved in the publication of the conventional book edition. Profits would not be built into the pricing structure of any publication, electronic or hard. Ultimately, this special edition, whether electronic or hard, of Fox's "The Fairy Queen", has an actually 'planned' place in two of the full volumes of Fox's poetry to be published in due course. It is, in fact, a poem that was originally written to fit into volume two of his work titled "Inscriptions"[21], it also fits into volume one titled "English Wounds".

---

promised of "The Fairy Queen" when repeatedly printed, except in so far as each book is differentiated by being written on by Fox himself in his own hand. Each book that Fox thus writes on becomes more clearly not only a 'different' object, but an 'individual' object. Bitzan created books as unique non-verbal objects containing hidden pulses of confined carnal energy, exposing to the light of observation their powers of telling, of ordering, bringing them forth from an Eco-like 'library', that fiery infestation of light found in the depths of "The Name of the Rose", wherein mysterious and murderous objects are managed by secret conclaves that preserve and conserve them for the library that holds them in its passionate, disordered breast.

[20] I take this from Fox's poem "oasis" (volume 7 "The Charred Lord") where he contends with such 'reality' problematics as 'cyberspace' ("Neuromancer" William Gibson, 1986), by considering the 'nature' of (an) oasis in terms of seeing one for real. It seems to me that Fox 'sees' actual objects and virtual objects as 'being' both merely phenomena, as it were timeless phantasmagoria, etymologically speaking.

[21] In Fox's "Inscriptions", there is a group of poems which include "The Fairy Queen" along with "Charles III", "Princess Diana", and "Lord Louis".

Fox's "Fairy Queen" is an exceptional attempt to express how it is that Mrs Elizabeth[22] Mountbatten[23] (Windsor), a shy, little lady in love with her husband Philip the Duke, a lady of unobtrusive but steely personality, now entering her late seventies, holds what seems to be an inexplicable grip on the seemingly irrational feelings of the British peoples and other peoples the world over. Fox's understanding of this extraordinary phenomenon is deep and is sympathetic to her and to the monarchy, and to the people so affected; he does not regard it as an inconsequential, simple matter to be bandied about as a mere entertainment. As so often with Fox's work, it may be easy to rush over the poem as if it were merely an entertaining trial or toadying tribute, or satirical swipe

---

[22] Elizabeth, is, according to Brewer's, from the Hebrew *Elîsaba*, 'my God gave the oath'; which is somewhat appropriate to Elizabeth II; not only in terms of her personal commitment, but in terms of her Coronation anointment by appeal to the authority of the Old Testament "Zadok" the High Priest of David and Solomon, and a court intriguer of the first order, according to Arthur Peake's "Commentary on the Bible", Jack, 1931. The Coronation 1902 edition of the Anglican Book of Common Prayer, is replete with formal reference to Zadok the priest and Nathan the prophet which carried over to the 1953 coronation of Elizabeth II.

[23] Ben Pimlott, "The Queen", Harper Collins 1996: pages 183-186 on Queen Mary's petty intrigue (not at all intimated by Pope-Hennessy in his 1959 biography "Queen Mary"), and on Churchill's petty if human hatred of Lord Mountbatten in 1952, etc; and page 270 where Philip continues to be bitter on this; and 297-299 when Prime Minister Harold Macmillan agrees to the name Windsor-Mountbatten being available at least to Prince Andrew and Edward. The point of this is that, having been overawed by Churchill, but subsequently realising the depth of her husband's feelings about his name being cast aside, the Queen tried, with some success, to resolve the matter through her excellent relationship with Macmillan in 1959.

at the obvious, or mere silly braggadocio[24] whose vapid airs infest an already much contaminated biosphere. This would be to miss the journey Fox makes back and forth through the nine by nine stanzas questing the layers of meanings that armour him, a modern day wandering knight errant, against the attack of the trivial. These notes should not be treated as some kind of cardboard ciborium and holy grail[25] wherein *the*

---

[24] Obscure reference (Silly Bragg) to the equally obscure and silly Billy Bragg. An example of the silly and popular of the present day who infest the British media pond where benighted pop stars are free to float around displaying trite left wing credentials as if on rings through their peckers. Not less obscure but perhaps of more significance is the reference to Spenser's "Faerie Queene", in keeping with his dislike for the 'Italian' character and the corrupting influence of the 'tour' on the young bloods which Spenser felt led to a serious decline of values, a loss of 'courtesy'. Chambers gives, *braggadocio* as: boasting, boaster, a name coined by Spenser, 1590, for a character personifying boastfulness in "The Faerie Queene".

[25] Grail: etymologically there is some interesting variation in how this word comes about. Skeat points out that: "the Holy Dish at the Last Supper. (F.=L.=Gk.) The etymology was very early falsified by an intentional change from *San Greal* (Holy Dish) to *Sang Real* (Royal Blood, perversely taken to mean Real Blood) = O.F. *graal, Greal, Grasal*, a flat dish; with numerous other forms, both in O.F. and Low L. It would appear that the word was corrupted in various ways from Low L. *cratella*, a small bowl, dimin. of crater, a bowl; see Crater". However, Brewer's gives Holy Grail: "According to medieval legend, the name is that of the bowl used by Jesus at the Last Supper, in which Joseph of Arimathea received Christ's blood during the Crucifixion. Joseph is said to have brought the cup to Glastonbury, when it became the quest of many knights, and especially King Arthur's knights of the Round Table. It is known by the alternative name of *Sangrail* or *Sangreal*, as if from the Old French *sang Graal*, (literally 'blood cup') 'Holy Grail'. *Grail* itself may have originated from medieval Latin *gradalis*, '*bowl*', a word that is perhaps related to Greek *kratér* (modern English *crater*), the term for a bowl in which wine and water were mixed

'meaning' of the poem is packaged, to be found and supped, and then conveniently disposed. The poem is both the grail and ciborium to be supped at, not these notes.

He has carefully shaped a poem with a very formal structure of nine rhymed stanzas of nine lines each in a reduced pentameter (four-five feet) style with occasional extension of the ninth (sometimes eighth as well) line to Alexandrine (hexameter, six feet). The structure is deliberately designed to bring Edmund Spenser's "Faerie Queene"[26] to mind. This wonderful poem, written over a period between the mid 1580s and

---

before being poured into cups. Some, however, have linked the word with Medieval Latin *gradale*, 'by degrees', 'by stages' (from classical Latin *gradus*, 'step'), as if applied to a dish or platter that was brought to the table at various stages of a meal. Others, on the other hand, have derived the word either from Medieval Latin *gradualis*, modern English gradual, as a sung portion of the Roman Catholic mass, or even from Irish *críol*, 'basket', 'casket' (English *creel*)." Of course, the key source, from a literary point of view, remains that of Jessie L Weston's "From Ritual to Romance", originally CUP, 1920, here Anchor Books edition, 1957. Grail is for holding the blood of Christ while 'ciborium' is to hold the flesh of Christ in the form of bread. Also see below the Gundestrup Cauldron.

[26] The Faerie Queene, Brewer's, 1992, gives a useful summary: "Spenser's famous poetic work, with the first three books published in 1590 and the second three in 1596, does not have a title that refers to a 'fairy queen' in the modern sense but to a 'queen of fairyland'. The word fairy (from Old French *faerie*) originally meant 'land of fays', a *fay* being an individual fairy. Spenser revived the medieval word as the name of the complex allegorical world described in his work, which has no 'fairies' in the popular sense. When the Introduction to Book II refers to the 'lond of Faery' it thus means 'land (that has the name) of fairy'. The *Faerie Queene* herself is Gloriana, a blend of the abstract concept Glory and a concrete evocation of Queen Elizabeth". 'Glory', although Ayto gives etymology unknown, Skeat finds root in 'KRU', Sanskrit *to hear* (?), Chambers does not go to root.

1596, is a great pre-modern allegorical 'novel' written in English in a highly structured poetic form now known eponymously as the Spenserian stanza.

This huge, unwordprocessed work is truly awesome. Its form, diction, numerology, the logical intricacy of its linguistic machinations, its range and depth of ideas, and the gripping, dramatic nature of the sci-fi adventures of its narrative, all beautifully conspire to create an exciting story, cinematic in process, that explores his then-world by wandering and wondering amongst its moral rocks and islands[27], those shifting sands and moral grounds upon which he founded "The Faerie Queene". There seems little doubt that Spenser had a quite definite moral purpose in mind that guided him through the writing of his "Queene". He was constructing a complete and comprehensive moral almanac to guide his peers, his fellow mortals through the general muddle of error that confounds the true observation of good in the everyday world.

Let me not pretend to a capacity to summarise the 75,000 lines of "The Faerie Queene" to provide you with a sound bite that encapsulates its whole point in one tasty, digestible pill; but, in essence, Spenser says there is a human behaviour named 'courtesy' which is good, and that by following this moral code of behaviour you will actually be good. But, what is this moral code 'courtesy' you ask? Indeed! Well, there are approximately 75,000 lines of explanation, formed in nearly 8,000 highly structured stanzas, in 72 cantos, in 6 books[28]. Thus, the question is begged as to why

---

[27] Compare "wandring Islands", with Homer's wandering Rocks. See in Paul J Alpers, "Edmund Spenser", Penguin Critical Anthologies, 1969, Martha Craig, page 337.

[28] Spenser's plan seems to have been for the production of 12 books "Fashioning XII Morall Vertues", thus, 150,000 lines, in 16,000 stanzas of 144 cantos. Wow!

Spenser needed 75,000 complex lines of verse to explain what 'good' is, when one sound bite will do?

It seems to me he is not explaining what good is, he assumes we know, but that he is explaining what the endless hazards and obstructions to goodness are and how, through awareness, we may navigate them skilfully, competently. What he is attempting to explain, or describe, are the rigours of effective 'moral competence'[29] in a world where the purely good are subject to so many and various and subtly tempting and attractively deceptive courses of error that easily lead to the pious self-deception that all is for the best come what may.

---

[29] The term 'moral competence' was originated by Fox in the English political arena in 1978 to distinguish between the natural tendency for most 'good' people to agree on this or that being morally good or bad; war is a bad thing; killing anyone at all is a bad thing; nuclear weapons are a bad thing; and such other easy mouthings; the widespread tendency is to conflate feeling good, or looking good, with being good. However, Fox argued then, and continues to argue, that feeling good is not enough, that it is incumbent on those claiming the moral high ground to think through how the 'goodness' they agree on is to be achieved. Many, often nauseatingly pompous and pious people, who present themselves to the world at large as good, fail miserably to see through their goodness with ways and means that are sufficient in the least to the support and achievement of that good they espouse. Such 'moral incompetents' are often, but not always, easily recognised because they commonly arrogate to themselves the right to exempt their 'good' objective from any serious analysis of their ways and means. The position they have taken is so 'good' that it cannot be argued with, and any question of moral competence is treated as an attack on the inherent, the self-evident 'goodness' of the objective they espouse. The fact that they have no serious idea how to achieve such an objective, of how to follow through the consequences, intended and unintended, seems always subservient to the obvious need for a transfer of substantial funds from others to support their cause.

Fox has altered the Spenserian stanza ababbcbcc rhyme scheme to spread the acoustic thus: abacbcdbd giving a royal thread bbb through each stanza drawn through by aba cbc dbd, creating three 'triplets' that read almost as traditional couplets, but spoiled a line onwards each time to find both completion and forward dynamic. As is widely recognised, Spenser was up to something quite different with his eponymous stanza,

> The great space of the [Spenserian] stanza makes it well suited to detailed narration and description. It is constructed as to bring to mind, and breath, almost to fatigue and then to force a rest before one goes on to the following stanza. [30]

The Alexandrine 9th line closure (hexameter, 12 syllable line) is breathtaking and gives pause to gather one's bearings.

The Spenserian three rhyme stanza structure is stretched by Fox to a four rhyme structure[31]. This achieves two effects. First, the pressure to find so many rhymes within one stanza of thought is reduced, thus allowing Fox much more freedom of manœuvre in pursuing decisive ambiguity[32] and overlaid imagery in his "Fairy Queen". Second, the stanzas are opened out sufficiently to ensure that they become less episodic,

---

[30] Karl Shapiro & Robert Beum, "A Prosody Handbook", Harper & Row, 1965, pages 124-5. This expresses the conventional view of what Spenser was up to with his extraordinary prosodic invention. Shapiro and Beum go on to point out the way the nature of the rhyme scheme suits the hugeness of Spenser's vision, commenting that the final 'couplet' refers back to the sixth line 'c' rhyme.

[31] This 'stretch' does not disrupt Fox's trinitarian numerology because it results in triplets comprising the nine lines of each stanza. Thus, the magical form of the poem is not simply uninterrupted, but is strengthened.

[32] See the introduction to Fox's "Songs of Nocence", for definition of 'decisive ambiguity'.

less discrete units of thought in a vast pattern, thus allowing the integrity of the nine stanzas and 81 lines as a whole to emerge unscathed by the lesser disjunction of narrative breathtaking at each stanza end prior to continuance of a long, complex, (Spenserian) allegorical story line. It also avoids the concomitant distortion of syntax to get rhyme right through to the end.

Thus, Fox is referring to Spenser, but is not writing 'spenserish'. The great Spenserian stanza, taking Empson here[33], is not required by Fox to carry us across a vast moral discursion, but is required for the aura of its era, for its roots, rather than to take off its "enormous patterns". Thus, Fox's "Fairy Queen" stanzas, unlike Spenser's, are full of "devices of implication". Fox relies on, the "lightning flashes of ambiguity", on concentrated cogs of poetic energy rather than the vast wheels of Spenserian dispersion.

Fox's "Fairy Queen" is allegorical in its reference to "The Golden Bough"[34], though it is not a use of allegory such as in an extended mythological 'code' of "Faerie Queene" proportions requiring an hermeneutic approach to discover the true 'plot' of the poet. Fox tends to the view that such abstruse 'plotting' may have been instinctive in times when even such a canny and powerful friend and patron as Sir Walter Raleigh, 1552-1618, could end up in perpetual imprisonment and thence, through events, to the block

---

[33] William Empson, op cit, page 54.
[34] James George Fraser, abridged from 1924 version "The Illustrated Golden Bough", 1996 edition, The Softback Preview. Fox is sensitive to the "bow-wow" charge that use of the Golden Bough material is hackneyed since T S Eliot's key references in "The Wasteland", 1922. However, he believes that there is an essential truth in the work which does reach beyond the Elizabethan, Anglo-Saxon and Roman to the deeper, pagan roots of the British, and that these roots still feed the present day collective psyche.

at Whitehall. He feels that political correctness has been a factor in the cunning[35] of true poets since the earliest times, even back unto the times when poets orated in the presence of their kings and within immediate reach of the sword that 'protected' them. Even today, the unwary poet may be confined to the garret[36] or mere niche in the wall of poetical correctness that bricks the free thinkers of the present time into unfunded obscurity. However, this would be to treat Spenser's method as deliberate obfuscation designed to protect him from standing accused of his 'true' meanings, rather than poetic machinery carefully constructed to form meanings he wished to extract or excise from his thought and lay in peculiar shape before the readers who knew him.

In this regard such poetic paranoia may be somewhat exaggerated by Fox's own naturally secretive nature and could be discounted to a large extent. However, there does seem good ground for Martha Craig's[37] view that there is more to Spenser's use of

---

[35] Cunning, according to Ayto, is close to 'canny', 13th century: *cunning* did not always have its present-day negative connotations. At first it was a term of approval, meaning 'learned'. It is connected in some way to the verb *can*, which originally meant 'know', although it is not altogether clear whether it is a direct use of the present participle of the English verb, or whether it was borrowed from the related Old Norse *kunnandi*, present participle of *Kunna* 'know'. Either way, it is a parallel formation to canny [16th Century]. The sense 'skilfully deceitful' developed towards the end of the 16th century.

[36] Garret, the etymology is helpful: OE *werian*, to defend (Hayward & Sparkes, 1968), allied to wary (Skeat). A case in point in regard to Martha Craig's argument about the secret wit of Spenser, below.

[37] Martha Craig, from, "The Secret Wit of Spenser's Language", in "Edmund Spenser", edited Paul J Alpers, Penguin Critical Anthologies, 1969, pages 322-339. An illuminating essay.

quaint, curious and archaic language, of purposelessly distorted words, peculiar coinages, empty decoration and other such opacities of the inkhorn than mere idiosyncrasy. Craig is convincing when she presents Spenser as the poet-dialectician and unravels the Platonic etymological[38] argument that inheres in the Cratylus of Plato. She reports:

> In the Cratylus Socrates sets forth the view that words must be not merely conventional and arbitrary, so many believe, but in fact 'correct' and 'true'. For if there is such a thing as reality and knowledge of it, our statements must be about reality, and they must be true to it. And if statements as a whole are to be true, the parts, that is, the words of which they are composed, must be true as well. Or, on the analogy of a craft like weaving or cutting, speaking is an action performed for a certain purpose and must be done not according to our own opinion or arbitrary whim but according to nature. We must have the proper instrument correctly suited to the task. In the craft of weaving, the instrument is the shuttle used to separate the web. In the craft of speaking, the instrument is the word.[39]

By implication this view of the poet's craft depends on a philosophical perspective that enables the naming of things to be done as if the names stood for or regarded 'a' reality, and here Fox is at one with the vatic Wittgensteinian conceipt[40] that:

---

[38] Etymology, according to Ayto 1990, has the underlying meaning from the Greek *étumos* 'real, true', coming to mean in the 16th century 'true or literal sense of a word'.
[39] Martha Craig, op cit, page 325.
[40] Conceipt, used by Spenser extensively. Does he mean conceit(ed) concept (?), which might turn out to be, perhaps, somewhat appropriate to Wittgenstein, rather than merely 'imagination, fancy', as given by my 19th century Spenser glossary.

57. "Something red can be destroyed, but red cannot be destroyed, and that is why the meaning of the word 'red' is independent of the existence of a red thing."—Certainly it makes no sense to say that the colour red is torn up or pounded to bits. But don't we say " The red is vanishing"? And don't clutch at the idea of our always being able to bring red to our mind's eye even when there is nothing red any more. That is just as if you chose to say that there would still always be a chemical reaction producing a red flame.—For suppose you cannot remember the colour any more?—When we forget which colour this is the name of, it loses its meaning for us; that is, we are no longer able to play a particular language-game with it. And the situation then is comparable with that in which we have lost a paradigm which was an instrument of our language.[41]

This is to say that words 'make up' the phenomenal as a mental objectification. The poet-dialectician, Fox, is constructing such an object with a dialectic of poetry-words (the right instrumentation to make something worth 'looking' at) in the shape of a finished poem. "The Fairy Queen", is such a finished object, sculpted (shaped[42]) to offer the reader (whose mind's eye has a seeing of it) endlessly available views[43] of the 'same'

---

[41] Ludwig Wittgenstein, "Philosophical Investigations", Translated by G E M Anscombe, Basil Blackwell, 1968, page 28^e

[42] Shape: this could serve as an excellent example of an etymological pun: being both OE *scóp* meaning poet (to shape words into a tale, see Pollington 1993); and through Skeat AS *sceapan, scapen*, pt. t. *scop* ff. being to shape. Ayto 1990 says shape is ultimately rooted in the pre-historic German base *skap* meaning form, create; then chop or scoop out a hole in the ground.

[43] Views here includes 'perspectives' in the sense: "His [Nietzche's] recognition of the importance of engaging in and drawing upon a multiplicity of such analyses in philosophical

thing. It is the poet's craft to make the 'samenesses' of it, and it is the reader's, the seer's, to see as many samenesses[44] as possible. In such 'viewings' of the poem as a mental phenomenon, the 'sameness' of the object, with its endless selves, cannot be seen as such, only supposed; whereas the views of 'it' seem to recur (supposedly), but are never the same as such; this is

---

inquiry is reflected in his insistence that such inquiry is inescapably perspectival—and that this circumstance is by no means fatal to it, if one can learn to capitalise upon the possibility of bringing a variety of perspectives to bear upon many of the matters with which it may concern itself." (from page 620, "The Oxford Companion to Philosophy", ed Ted Honderich, entry under Nietzche Fredrich, OUP, 1995).

[44] Here Fox has been at pains to let me know that his 'samenesses' are not quite Nietzchean in the way of Karl Löwith, though perhaps tinted (or tainted) by Nietzsche's successful conflation of time as a (real) cosmological dimension, rather than, according to Fox, a mere psychologism that, like Zeno's tortoise, we should ignore the impossibilities of surpassing, no matter our thoughts move with the speed of arrows. The Nietzsche problematic, Fox thinks, is very much to do with his 'poetic' (*poiesis,* action, way of transforming into poetry) having a philosophic character that is merely apparently philosophical, but being actually schizoidal; thus, we are easily (mis)led to produce two explanations of everything Nietzche wrote expecting them to be ultimately compatible. When it comes to Fox, in the way of views of *the*, or *a*, poem being object, the 'sameness' of such objectification as phenomenal sculpture cannot be in itself seen, only necessarily supposed. Thus, the whole, while always in mind, is always necessarily incomplete because there are infinite different ways in which such an object can be viewed. The true art of the poet is to create a shape that is worthy of infinite viewings. This aspect of Fox's thinking involves a reading of Karl Löwith's, "Nietchze's Philosophy of the Eternal Recurrence of the Same", translated by J Harvey Lomax, and with a key forward by Bernd Magnus, University of California Press, 1978.

because the seer, when 'seeing', has them in mind as one and the same.

Wittgenstein's situation of the loss of a paradigmatic instrument of language is perhaps the converse or contrary state to Spenser's attraction to the paradigmatic source of words' 'true' meanings through etymological reconstruction (or reference). Fox 'sees' the Wittgensteinian point within his own observation that:

> In languages other than English it is often the case that any specific colour is observed differently being named over different divisions of the electromagnetic spectrum of light (a continuum across 380-780 nanometres.); therefore, colours are a good example of the way names invent observation. Thus, 'red' is cultured (cultivated) in our minds by a necessarily antecedent educative perceptual process.[45]

Thus, the 'idea' that words are somehow independent instruments of meaning, that words have (or are) 'referential meanings-in-themselves', is wrong. Words are histories of experience defined by use, by the way they have been and are played in games where they are involved. Such histories are recorded in the etymologies of each word, even of such glorious mistakings as Christopher Ricks' "beresk"[46] moment, not a word apparently deserving an etymological existence, yet it carries over 'bereft', 'burlesque', 'grotesque' in the rush of 'berserk', giving their etymologies a chance to fertilise error and thence, perhaps, to thrive. In this mood Fox has resurrected

---

[45] This is actually a pencilled annotation on page 28^e of Fox's own copy of Wittgenstein's "Philosophical Investigations", op cit.

[46] Christopher Ricks, "Word Making and Mistaking", in "The State of the Language", Edited by Christopher Ricks and Leonard Michaels, University of California Press, 1990, page 461.

the subterranean "glistered" (stanza 7), the now obsolete form of 'glittered', which has the effective resemblance and advantage of a new word "unbeknownst", as Ricks put it, but which actually carries over a 'history' waiting to be unearthed by anyone willing to dig for it.

If all words ultimately return to one root word, then 'The' Word (Logos), can be taken as 'The Word of God', or the first word 'UG'. Such an oral gesture (UG) was perhaps hastily adapted to 'Guh' 'Guh' 'Guh', expressed in the context of expansive non-verbal gesture, being the first, second and third words by which the semiotic imperative 'everything' was said of, was placed in suspended semiosis; the first word being revelatory, the second and third words (Guh) being The Voice's teaching, the inculcation of everything. Once having said everything including the inculcation, 'Guh' became practically useless, being somewhat a blunt instrument, though clearly establishing the owner of the word 'Guh' as controlling access to Guh (God-everything its word-of), the keeper of 'The' word 'Guh' (heris[47] first priest[48], the one who led others from the wilderness, the leader, the educator[49]). Thus, 'God is

---

[47] Fox has introduced the pronoun simplification *heris*, pronounced as spelt and to mean 'her &/or his'. This also conveniently disposes argument about the gender of deity, by avoiding the linguistic gender trap built into the English language and its snare of designating a deity in the masculine or neuter. Is God an he or an 'it'? Or, following the use of 'gender' in linguistics to mean 'kind', is deity akin not to sex but some other class of existence; or is 'heris' in a separate class, neither male nor female nor neuter, but 'heristic', a purely metaphysical entity?

[48] Priest, according to Ayto, is 'elder', Greek *presbútos*. It is, of course, s/he who outlives that has the ultimate voice, the last word about the first.

[49] Educate, according to Ayto, Skeat, Chambers, is to literally 'lead them out', L *ēducāre*.

UG'[50] (not dead[51], but derived from the first 'voicing', *guth*[52]).

Such monopoly of god through a grabbing of 'The' word led, it seems, to the hubris of the Tower of Babel, and the inevitable deserts of the fall. This metaphor is described by Rod Mengham in the opening to his book "The Descent of Language":

> The Tower of Babel. The idea of this building, which has gripped the imagination of artists and writers for thousands of years, represents both the pinnacle of linguistic ambition and the height from which real languages are judged to have fallen. The crazy attempt to erect a structure that might bridge the gap between earth and heaven shows the depth and intensity of human need, the need to be furnished with a language that not only matches the world of

---

[50] To the linguist the 'UG' theory, although crude, assumes *homo loquens*, 'speaking man' The conventional view (and linguists are the ultimate conventionalists) is that no theory explains the origin of language. But then this is to ask too much. David Crystal's "The Cambridge Encyclopedia of Language", 1987, page 289, gives groupings of the possible theories. He amusingly lists Jespersen's grouping of five commonly held theories: the "bow wow" theory; the "pooh pooh" theory; the "ding dong" theory; the "yo-he-ho" theory; the "la-la" theory. 'UG' comes closest to the "ding dong" theory which can be summed up as deriving from oral gesture. However, this does not seem adequate and one is left with the impression that the linguists continue dryly on a narrow beach, toes undipped, unobserving the sea. Of course, how you get from 'UG' to English, as here being used, is not easily explained (by a linguist).

[51] Friedrich Nietzche, 1844-1900, "God is Dead", is taken from "The Gay Science", or as I prefer 'The Joyful Science' ("Die Fröhlich Wissenschaft", III, 108):

> God is dead: but considering the state the species of Man is in, there will perhaps be caves, for ages yet, in which his shadow [Schatten] will be shown [zeigt].

[52] 'Voice", Old Irish *guth* 'voice' (Brewer's), Sanskrit *vach* 'to speak' (Skeat), or Indo European *wek* 'speak', 'say' (Ayto).

> physical phenomena, but which in some sense brings that world into existence. In the language of God, words have creative power, and the biblical formula 'In the beginning was the Word' suggests the extent to which consciousness of the world only springs into being with the utterance, or inscription, of those words that give us names for it.
>
> The descent from the Tower, then, is like another Fall: a decline into anarchy and linguistic isolation. And yet the instant of chaos in the biblical myth stands for nothing less than the whole of human history, for the process of gradual divergence, and occasional re-convergence, of multifarious linguistic traditions.[53]

That Babel should appear as a punishment, a descent, is of biblical origins wherefrom, of course, much error is derived. The breaking up of 'UG' is better seen as an ascent from the confines of monolinguism to the open spaces of the multilingual, the dissemination of the seeds of free thought through open languages between peoples.

Before the biblical word, of language-enslaved, there was the being purely expressed until fixed by the Book. Such pure power, given unto the pre-emptive speaker of a proto-language, the first being of it, when there was none among the tribe of them before would have seemed well worth worshipping. Thus, those who formed language in their mouths, the blood of tongues, and who pointed the sounds of it that they had made in their mouths with their whole bodies, were the then

---

[53] Rod Mengham, "The Descent of Language", Bloomsbury Publishing, 1993, page 3. Here Mengham does not distinguish between 'THE word' and 'the WORD', which leaves aside much of interest.

superhuman[54]. They were the first prophets who knew the future through the words of their minds. They could manipulate the entire perceptible universe beneath their tongues, though their opened mouths seemed empty of any visible, tangible object, but were full of invisibilities, the intangible words themselves whose untestable truth was real, but untouchable, yet tasty in the mouths that heard them, the ears that savoured their first, fresh tang.

In Pinker's[55] world it is the language gene that yields Darwin being able to write "The Origin of Species", and we being able to read it, even to instinctively understand it, certainly being able to entertain argument with it, even to play politics with it. Is this gene an exceptional gift from God, or is the word 'god' simply 'UG' by another name? And as they spoke out of their nature of unique entities ('uniquities'[56]), so such became visible in their own minds. These mental visibilities ('visimentals'[57])

---

[54] Superhuman, den Übermenschen, overman, superman, Friedrich Nietzche's, "Thus Spake Zarathustra", prologue, 1883:
> I teach you the superman. Man is a thing to be surmounted [Überwinden, surpass]. What have ye done to surmount him?
> All beings hitherto have created something above themselves: will ye be the ebb of this great tide and rather revert to the beast than surpass man? What is the ape to man? A jest or thing of shame. So shall man be to Superman—a jest or a thing of shame.

[55] Steven Pinker, "The Language Instinct", Penguin Books, 1994.

[56] An 'uniquity' is a Rousseaun object, see below. The several coinages here are from Fox's 'frontier thinking', justified, he says, in the way of T S Eliot's "... the poet is occupied with frontiers of consciousness beyond which words fail, though meanings still exist."

[57] 'Visimentals' are not restricted to mere images, but include all thought that is 'seen'.

goaded their bodies to make their speech visible, and to 'really' preserve it that it stayed distinct and continuing (an 'existinctual'). These 'representations,' as it were 'existentualisations', of the 'uniquities' as they emerged into view, re-inscribed on their minds, minds whose instinctual sharp points wrote their speech out of themselves, made their speech visible. The problematic of an 'uniquitous' universe is that the mathematics of 'uniquities' no more assumes division, does not permit more than one things-in-mind. The familiar inevitability of binarisation in thought cannot be sustained, except as mere psychologism. No more this or that, true or false, now or then, here or there. In an 'uniquitous' universe language detaches itself from the psychology humankind, the mere psyche of the individual or tribe. The language of number depends entirely on the economics of doing business, the need to count the money (grain, cattle, gems and all such objects of value in exchange).

Thus, the economics of language is the pure politics of survival. Naming is owning, is controlling the valuable objects in scope. And language is nothing but naming everything, dividing 'world' ('that' into 'this') into anarchic name after name after name and bringing them under tactical control, marshalling the forces of such running words like wild horses[58] under the rein of syntactic rule, the priest grammarian, the monarchical[59] speech, the Queen's English, while rebellious pronouncers, the subverters, spit the bits slavering from their mouths, as if letting their mouths run free is freedom of speech. Most of all, people are

---

[58] Horse, the etymology is interesting in that through various branches it is possible to trace horse back through OE and through Latin to *currere* to 'run' (Ayto, Skeat), and thus (Fox) to going 'fast', thus to the power of speed and its harnessing.
[59] Monarch, 'meaning one ruler' (Greek, Latin, OE, Skeat et al); cf anarchy.

named and known and placed. Who knows the most names have the potential necessary power to manage the most people.

But 'UG', the first word, is ONE involving its speaker in the 'that', while 'Guh' cannot but dis-involve its speaker from the 'that'. Thus, dividing to rule is irresistible, each new word a missile in mouths hungry for power, surely the very first splitting[60] when mouth bit at all of 'that' (its 'world') and spat out the bits by taste; thereof a vast bird rose heading for the tower top, heaven, regurgitating food for thought and between meals speaking of Rousseau:

> Every object at first received a particular name without regard to genus or species, which these primitive originators were not in a position to distinguish; every individual presented itself to their minds in isolation, as they are in the picture of nature. If one oak was called A, another was called B; for the primitive idea of two things is that they are not the same ...[61]

Such 'uniquitous' in-distinction is very much more a problem for mathematics than verbal language as such. The mathematical problem becomes critical in, for

---

[60] Split, the etymology is fascinating in providing at this point the precise word (instrument) to explain the impossible, that by splitting (dividing) the vast 'that' into bits of 'this-esses' and 'that's', the effect ultimately is to join the bits (splice) all together. Whether this is chaotic (chaos theory provides that unpredictability is not the same as randomness) or orderly is merely relative between the predictable and the unpredictable.

[61] I am grateful to Lawrence Attree's unpublished 2002 paper "Paradox and Obstruction in Rousseau's Social Theory", which drew my attention to this thought of Rousseau's, referenced as "The Second Discourse", page 67, J-J Rousseau, "Essay on the Origin of Languages and Writings Related to Music: Collected Writings of Rousseau", Vol 7, Edited and Translated by J Scott, Hanover, UP of New England, 1998. In this regard Rousseau is right, no two things are the same.

example, Monostone's[62] consideration of the nature of nothing, of dimensionless space, the unextended object. This is to treat mathematics as a non-verbal "mentalese"[63] whereof numbers, except the first one, are protean in their many forms of being not 'words' about objects, but the morphemics of mental phenomena. Thus, the seemingly innate desire to rebuild the great tower reaching even unto the heaven of true understanding, to return to the one heavenly word that says it all, no questions asked (back to UG?).

Craig develops Spenser's role as poet-dialectician to include using (exploiting) the nature of the 'experience' in words themselves, their etymologies, to reveal the nature of what is referred to. Words themselves are naturally subject to invention and development through connectivities with other words and their etymologies by visual, aural, linguistic, and other poetic dialectic (machination) that effectively associates them with other words and their concomitant etymologies. Ultimately 'true' meaning is a primary point, a non-verbal form within a sound envelope communing with its meaning, as it were: 'being-what-it-means'. The somewhat circular argument emerges that, according to Craig's view of Plato's Cratylus, the singular primary sound envelope 'UG' must be true, assuming it was 'UG' and not 'OG', and that we could somehow still 'perceive' the non-verbal form it acted within, though we can, of course, only ever 'imagine' such a perception.

---

[62] Albert Monostone, "Dear Zeno, about God's Sensorium", in progress.
[63] Steven Pinker, "The Language Instinct", Penguin, 1994, gives 'mentalese' as "The hypothetical 'language of thought,' or representation of concepts and propositions in the brain in which ideas, including the meanings of words and sentences, are couched.", page 478.

Of course, the built-in assumption that the first word was first said once by one voice[64] and then transmitted onwards to everyone else is a somewhat singular view of language most suited to those religiously inclined who have a natural tendency toward hierarchical authoritarianism; or indeed to that significant proportion of people who, Victor Vroom[65] concluded, were what he termed "high authoritarians" in modern western societies. By this his research

---

[64] Umberto Eco, "In Search For The Perfect Language", Basil Blackwell, 1995, Chapter 5 "The Monogenetic Hypothesis". Eco is pointing out that such a single origin for language gives some basis for the formation of a future common language (thus a perfect language, thus of constructing the tower of Logos up to heaven, that the language be god, thus inviting descent to Babel, the collapse of the over-ambitious tower yet again). Nevertheless, Eco's contention, page 116, is:

> Cavalli-Sforza's work on genetics (cf, for example 1988, 1991) tends to show that linguistic affinities reflect genetic affinities. This supports the hypothesis of a single origin of all languages, reflecting the common evolutionary origin of all human groups. Just as humanity evolved only once on the face of the earth, and later diffused across the whole planet, so language. Biological monogenesis and linguistic monogenesis thus go hand in hand and may be inferentially reconstructed on the basis of mutually comparable data.
>
> In a different conceptual framework, the assumption that both the genetic and the immunological codes can, in some sense, be analysed semiotically seems to constitute the new scientific attempt to find a language which could be defined as the primitive one *par excellence* (though not in historical but rather in biological terms). This language would nest in the roots of evolution itself, of phylogenesis as of ontogenesis, stretching back to before the dawn of humanity (cf. Prodi, 1977).

[65] Victor Vroom, I am working purely from memory here and cannot locate the 1960s research paper involved.

showed that a substantial proportion of people preferred being given clear instruction or directions, and did not like being left to their own devices, the remainder (about half of the sample), preferred being left to work things out for themselves and quickly resented being given what appeared to them as instructions or directions. In my experience this split seems to apply across the board in western societies.

Apart from the 'experience' inhering in words, their etymologies are defined by the actions they portray, by the games that they play. Thus, as Craig extends:

> In poetry the definition [of a word] is dramatised either literally or symbolically by the action. The meaning of 'Agamemnon'[66] in the view of classical and Renaissance commentators, is implicit in the etymology, but it is fully disclosed only in the action of the *Iliad*. The reader discovers the meaning of the name by analysing the action of the poem. Homer, with the aid of divine inspiration, originally discovered the proper, name, or true meaning of the given name by analysing the conduct of his character in life.[67]

Thus, for example, the demise of the English classical education of the public schools and Old Universities brought about the loss of a phylogenetic language game in common when the secret code between such fellows of the tribe went into the void.

That aside, we always have words in action, with their etymologies, and the ways and means of their uses in action, making-up their meanings right before us, coming to us movingly, living and breathing in our ears and acted out before our eyes. In this we are faced with the broader problem of an universal

---

[66] Agamemnon, after Craig, *agastos* meaning 'admirable', and *menein* 'enduring'; or after Brewer's 'very resolute'.
[67] Martha Craig, op cit, page 329.

language which Umberto Eco[68] describes in considering the perfect language of images when he points out the difficulties of dealing with "images for aliens". How are we to create a language in which we could warn a future generation of humankind grown wholly as alien to us as we to the ancient Egyptians, or indeed warn alien visitors to our planet, of our underground stores of deadly nuclear waste with a half life of thousands of years?

In this, Fox has come to a view close to Eco that the perfect language is the creation of a 'being' that is a continuing 'content' of languages, a meaning (story) in them that they merely carry, a narrative in them that they carry, the story which is conveyed and not the conveyances (the languages) themselves. Such conveyances are only incidental to 'The Story' itself. In the nuclear case, the story is the 'the myth of dragon tongue curled in its cave burning without feeling, unendingly. This is 'The Story' itself, the 'perfect language'. For Fox this means a story told through generations of poets, a continuing priesthood committed to the esoteric narrative of the unfeeling dragon. Such a priesthood could carry over the meanings 'in words' that are in themselves ever extending, but unbroken etymological narratives. Thus, the languages may differentiate across huge shifts of sounds and transform syntactically, yet each elemental word of them comprising the current 'machinery of conveyance' would remain concatenate with their origins.

It is this that could provide Eco's "narrative solution" whereby, even though the words in themselves disappear as elements comprising any extant language, they survive as 'empty' narratives (or

---

[68] Umberto Eco, "The Search For The Perfect Language", Blackwell, 1995, chapter 7.

myths) inside later languages as symbiotic cyphers[69] of meaning that can be uncoded to carry over the original 'story' of the nuclear hazard lurking in those places where evil sits in his dark cave waiting the intrusion of light, a deadly dragon radiating unfeeling fire.

Thus, though the way 'the unfeeling dragon' is conveyed may be ephemeral, yet the story itself, however it manifests itself at any point, is a metaphor revealed through the unearthing of the elemental wordage of the language currently sustaining it. Thus, the dragon, like a butterfly, is ever dependent on linguistic ephemera to lift it from time to time. So it rides into the ever present on the tips of tongues. In this, the internal consistency of poetic form, in terms of the universal and continuing, monogenetic nature of poetics and the mathematical character of their tautologies, as of music, is not, according to Fox, eschewed by the passage of time. On the contrary it is ever confirmed by the inevitable metaphorical nature of every form of human communication, albeit that the object of metaphor is never what it seems or that 'UG' when 'logogrammed &/or phonogrammed' and reduced to its multiplicity of differentials cannot be less than the story it is telling.

In any case, in considering the form in which to release the wordage of his 'narrative', Fox felt that mimicking exactly the Spenserian stanza would produce a ponderousness out of keeping with 'cybennial'[70] times. Thus, he devised the 'stripped-

---

[69] According to Ayto, 'cipher' is from Arabic *sifr* 'zero', through Old French and L. Cipher etymologically means 'empty'. Gullberg, 1997, gives Hindu *sunya* meaning 'void', 'emptiness'. Thus, their presence as empty 'words' is to beg the question of their missing histories to be found therein.
[70] 'Cybennial', an inkhorn term (new coinage), originally made in an editorial comment on Albert Smith's draft "utterance of the true thing of it that is" to describe the post-postmodern character of Smith's work. A 'definition' can be

down' form used here, but without loss of genetic code. He has his "Queen" emerge in an highly formal poetic structure in keeping with the threefold nature of the British constitutional monarchy: as head of state; symbolic head of the British people; and as sacrificial individual[71] available for their perpetual consumption. He is also making a direct reference to Spenser's "Faerie Queene" as providing a general background colour or tone for his own "Queen".

However, the question of a numerology to Fox's "Queen" does not extend beyond the idea of threefoldedness, thus searches for *ninenesses* and *eighty-onenesses*, would not prove fruitful except in the traditional regard of nine as the divine number three[72]

---

found http://www.justwords.demon.co.uk follow justWords then Albert Smith then click cybennial.

[71] Spenser considered his Faerie Queene (Elizabeth I) as bearing two persons, "… she beareth two persons, the one of a most royal Queene or Empresse, the other of a most vertuous and beautifull lady, this latter part in some places I doe express in Belphœbe, fashioning her name according to your owne excellent conceipt of Cynthia: Phœbe and Cynthia being both names of Diana." (from "Letter of the Author's to Sir Walter Raleigh", 23rd January 1583). Fox has modernised this view to include the British monarch not only as Sovereign (constitutional role) and beautiful person (woman) but also to include her role as symbolic head of the nation (national symbol). The hint of Diana is not without relevance.

[72] Three, the divine number 3 of tradition is also, cybennially, the universal number D, that is the number of spatial dimensions in the universe as remarked and included by Martin Rees as one of the SIX numbers that govern the universe, see his "just six NUMBERS", Phoenix Paperback, 1999, page 3:

> The sixth crucial number has been known for centuries, although it is now viewed in a new perspective. It is the number of spatial dimensions in our world, D, and equals three. Life couldn't exist if D were two or four.

multiplied by itself being 9 the incorruptible number of completion and eternity[73]. Nine amplifies the sacred three as in the Kyrie Eleison (Lord have mercy[74]), whereof the Father, Son and Holy Ghost is a trinity woven through a ninefold expression. While the nine storey pagoda[75] is not quite what Fox had in mind, it exemplifies the nature of his 9 x 9 structure being reference to the mystical, the mysterious, the

---

[73] David Fontana, "The Secret Language of Symbols", Pavilion Books Limited, 1993, page 65. Fontana says "Nine is associated with the circle, the square and the triangle. For the Chinese, it was the celestial number the most auspicious of all, and there were nine great social laws and nine classes of officials. In Hinduism, nine squared produces the 81-square mandala (though 82 squares including itself), which symbolises the universe and is used as an aid in prophecy and in astrological calculations.

[74] Kyrie Eleison ("Lord have mercy"), see page 775, F L Cross, "The Oxford Dictionary of the Christian Church", OUP, 1958. The entry explains thus: "A brief prayer for Divine mercy which from an early date has been used in the liturgical worship of the Church. The use of the word in non-Christian cultus is also attested (cf. *Epictus, *Diss*. ii. 7). In Christian usage they appear to have originated in Syria in the 4th cent. and to have reached the S. of France by the 6th. In the E. it is a response made by the deacon to prayers and litanies offered by the celebrant, whereas in the W. it is used as an independent formulary, e.g. in the Roman Mass the celebrant repeats with the server three times the words 'Kyrie eleison", three times again 'Christe eleison', and three times again 'Kyrie eleison' (the three groups being conceived as directed to the Father, Son, and Holy Ghost respectively). In the Eucharistic rite of the BCP [Book of Common Prayer] of 1549, the Kyrie survived in an English translation ('Lord have mercy upon us'), but in 1552 the Ten Commandments were substituted and have been prescribed here ever since, though reversion to the use of Kyries has been widely adopted unofficially. Their use in an English form at *Mattins, *Evensong, and the *Litany has been continuous since 1549."

[75] Ubo Becker, "The Element Encyclopedia of Symbols", Element Books Limited, 1994, page 212.

mythological and heavenly aspiration. And this creates the overtone of high formality and the undertone of the mysterious forest life of early Britain with its druidic[76] culture of the oak, sacrifice and renewal, as is found in Spenser's "Faerie Queene".

Then there are the three extant promises of the coronation oath of the Anglo-Saxon Kings[77] to provide

---

[76] Druid: Fox has an idiosyncratic theory that this word is an etymological pun. Ayto gives the following which could be seen as "druid" meaning both truth sayer (sooth) and oak tree, an etymological 'pun', as it were. Ayto says: *Druid* is, not surprisingly, of Celtic origin, although English probably acquired it via French *druide* or the Latin plural *druides*. The source of these forms was Gaulish *druides*, which came ultimately from Old Celtic **derwíjes*. There are two opposing theories on the derivation of this: one is that it comes from an Old Celtic adjective *derwos* 'true' (source of Welsh *derw* 'true'), in which case its etymological meaning would be 'someone who says the truth' (a parallel formation to English *soothsayer*); the other is that it was formed from the Old Celtic base **dru-* 'tree' (source of Welsh *derwen* and Irish *daur* 'oak-tree' and related to Greek *drus* 'oak' and English *tree*) in reference to the central role played by oak-trees in druidic ceremonies.

[77] William A Chaney, "The Cult of Kingship in Anglo-Saxon England", Manchester University Press, 1970 [1999], pages 255-56. Essentially, the Anglo-Saxon kings (they that have, etymologically, 'kinship', are from the royal kin, family group) were, toward the end of the first millennium anno domini, in process of conversion from paganism, a sacrificial druidic animism and vegetation cult, to Christianity which was, as now, very similar in its basic characteristics, though perhaps somewhat more cannibalistic in its general inclination. Chaney reports that:

> Further, the coronation oath of the Anglo-Saxon king expresses the duty of a Christian monarch in three promises. These survive not only in Latin in the Pontifical of Egbert and in the coronation *ordo* for King Æthelred's coronation but in Anglo-Saxon, which 'is written, letter by letter, after the writing that Archbishop Dunstan delivered to our lord (King Edgar) at Kingston on the day that they hallowed

their people with: peace; justice; and mercy. Thus, Fox's folding numerology (of 3s) is a woven (social) fabric[78], comprised of the interlaces of the various

---

> him king (May 11th, A.D. 973)' [Cotton MS]. This brief *promissio regis*, which the king 'laid up on Christ's alter, as the bishop directed him', pledges three things: 'true peace' to the Church and people, the prohibition of 'robbery and all unrighteous things to all orders', and 'in all dooms [judgments] justice and mercy, that the gracious and merciful God of his everlasting mercy may forgive us all'.

[78] In developing the idea of social fabric in regard to the role of the crown in cybennial Britain I have been sensitive to the fact that Fox deliberately did not intermedle Sir Thomas Malory's unravelling of the vast Arthurian tapestries with the weave of Spenser's "Faerie Queene". He has pointed out to me specifically that he has been sensitive to Eugène Vinaver's 1954 (OUP) edition of "The Works of Sir Thomas Malory", and with particular reference to Vinaver's introduction page viii. Here Vinaver describes the way Malory unravelled his "Arthur" stories from the dense fabric of the French Arthurian prose cycle:

> It [the French Arthurian prose cycle] was an elaborate fabric whose growth and development had been achieved not by a process of indiscriminate expansion, but by means of a consistent lengthening of each thread. Malory's adaption, on the other hand, was far from possessing or even attempting the unity which is claimed for it by the critics. He never tried to reduce his French romances to 'one story'; the method he used was both more subtle and more drastic. With great consistency, though with varying degrees of success, he endeavoured to break up the complex structure of his sources and replace their slowly unfolding canvas of recurrent themes by a series of self-contained stories. It was a delicate and difficult process of unravelling, of collecting the various stretches of any given thread and letting it unwind itself with as few interruptions as possible.

In this regard we may take Vinaver with Rosemary Tuve, 1966, and consider Fox's conclusion that Spenser, as a cybennial poet rather than a post-modernist, would perhaps

threefoldings of Royalty, and the Christian commitment of the Queen, and the Trinity itself as still a precious thread through her life and the established or otherwise extant British religious institutions whose various livings continue to find fertile grounds for drawing on dead wealth and the living. Fox's manyfold layering of threes upon threes being a nine ply royal fabric, a complex poem of cloth of gold, a royal poem, a realty, a reality.   Nine is the Anglo-Saxon King's number,

> Here in these laws we note the 'king's number', the nine of magic and folklore, which is used also to measure the sacral area of the king's peace, in the private treatise *grith*, extending three miles and three furlongs and three lineal acres and nine feet

---

have hypertexted his "Faerie Queene" to lay out both the weave of it and the weft of it as a 'de-formulated' fabric bearing the two dimensional image of his thought, and in so doing he may have succeeded in creating at least a three dimensional image as an phenomenal object observable in the mind's eye. In regard to Spenser's "Faerie Queene", Tuve observes with some precision:

> This structure [entrelacement] also is incorrectly termed episodic or repetitive or parallel, for the subtler effects and advantages here noted as typical or interlaced, not parallel, happenings will be seen to characterise any Book [of the "Faerie Queene"]the reader cares to examine closely.
>
> This web-structure has special possibilities of gradually discernible meaning as the woven pattern shows it *is* a pattern and *takes* shape. Hence it was a superbly invented instrument for conveying not only what we call the polyphonic nature of what is happening, but that which interested Spenser supremely, the fact that to human minds what happens 'means' something, is significant.

This thread of thought can be drawn through the eye of the Wittgensteinian needle to sew up the idea that meaning is made in moves.

and nine *scæftamunda* and nine barleycorns' [ref Pax, circa AD 910].[79]

The apparence that numbers, unlike words, are, according to Craig, "images simply of quantities", and cannot therefore be "perfected", is a common over-simplification. Indeed, it is a standard de-mystification of numbers by the *literati* as if numbers are not words. Ultimately, the true problematic of numbers, and consequently of all mathematics, is that numbers are apparently like words in referring to the concrete and that the concrete preceded the abstract. Thus, number as heterogeneous plurality in the concrete is distinct from number as a counting behaviour.

> It is counting that consolidated the concrete and therefore the heterogeneous notion of plurality, so characteristic of primitive man, into the *homogeneous abstract number concept*, which made mathematics possible.[80]

We move from Rousseau's primitive human to Einstein by counting. And it is by counting that we leave behind numbers as words in ordinary use, such as, the many ordinary words for the idea of 'two'[81] pair, couple, set, team, twin, brace, between, twine, duo.

Nevertheless, the problematic for mathematics must always remain that it is based upon the quintessential untruth that samenesses (kinds,

---

[79] William A Chaney, "The Cult of Kingship in Anglo-Saxon England: The Transition From Paganism To Christianity", Manchester University Press, 1970 [1999], page 215 ("Sacral Kingship in Anglo-Saxon Law").
[80] Tobias Dantzig, "Number: The Language of Science", Allen & Unwin 4th Edition, 1962, pages 6-7.
[81] Two, according to Ayto, is an ancient word traceable right back to the ancient Indo-European *duwo*. Skeat points out that 'two' had gender in the in AS [OE] which give us the origin of *two* and *twain*, there were masculine feminine and neuter forms of the number 'two', but now lost in '2'. This makes Dantzig's point clear.

categories) really exist ('are'); rather than being the mere inventions of perception, which are, in turn, perspectival, and thus human psychologisms. This can only resolve if man is made in the image of God, and God 'is'; thus, making human psychology universally significant, and therefore likewise mathematics. In this the foundation of mathematics would depend on god, which could suggest to we atheists that mathematics is little more than obscure if useful prayer, through which we entreat our minds to the comfort of following our first thought.

However, Craig is making the point, abstractly if not concretely, that:
> Words are only approximations, but as such, they can be perfected. Numbers, because they are images simply of quantities, cannot be; if we change II to III, we do not refer to the same number better, we refer to another number. But if we change 'demon' to 'dæmon', we improve the word and make it more revealing by showing more clearly the identity of spirit and intelligence.[82]

Fox is of the view that numbers, as Craig means, of abstraction, of counting, are something like morphemes, rather than words played out in ordinary language as such. Thus, in ordinary language numbers have etymologies such as,
> The number technique of many primitive peoples is confined to just such a matching and tallying [of one-to-one correspondence]. They keep the record of their herds and armies by means of notches cut in a tree or pebbles gathered in a pile. That our ancestors were adept in such methods is evidenced by the etymology of the words *tally* and *calculate*, of which the first comes from the Latin *talea*, cutting, and the second from the Latin *calculus*, pebble.[83]

---

[82] Martha Craig, op cit, page 328.
[83] Tobias Dantzig, op cit, page 7.

From such histories it can be readily understand that losing track of concrete things when they become mere cuts or pebbles is inevitable.

In this way number as the artifice of counting is a social product of exchange. It is about the wealth of herds and flocks, of gaggles and gatherings, of weighings and measurings, that form and reform in the chattering minds of humankind. There is thus a truly vast metaphorical shift from 'reality' to mathematical thought when identifiably different things become samenesses and lose their own peculiar identities to be carried over to find their ways into the universal tradings of mathematics on the eternal stock exchange of the 'same'. In this way all mathematics is essentially carried by metaphor, that something is else than itself. Thus, number as symbolic numerology in poetry need not be merely understood mathematically, but felt magically as to do with things seen in dreams.

It is noticeable in this regard that pentangular symbols, while pointedly bearing the apparently definite number five, and being already perfected, do not bear close scrutiny because they are composed of marriages of the feminine two and the masculine three. Such mathematical matrimony of the first two numbers of all numbers[84] gives five; noting that unity is not counted literally as a number, being the same as 'UG' the first word, that is ONE meaning everything. In this regard 'UG' is not a word. ONE is expressed as 'UG', and from 'UG' numbers are entities articulated by distinction. The fertility of the marriage of two and three makes the pentacle the ultimate numerological fertility symbol.

---

[84] The true numerologist would note at this point that the female (2) precedes the male (3), that Eve seems to precede Adam, that four is barren, that Abel the Pentacle is followed by the Cain the Hexagram. Such is the convincing 'logic' when numerology rules; yet such 'magic' feels convincing.

It is interesting that the classical pentacle symbol is seemingly comprised of two 'triangles' (pentagrammatically related), as it were interlaced (entrelaced or intermedled). It is not interwoven as the seal of Solomon (hexa-grammatically, Star of David), but as Celtic patterning interlaces neverendingly, like a 'straightsided circle'[85], and that without interlacing neverendingly the sides would generate six points and not five. The interlacing, the marriage of the five sides makes one three sided triangle and one two sided 'triangle'. This Escher-like[86] property or Möbius behaviour[87] introduces a form of dimensioning which leaves the 'normal' perspectival considerations thwarted, though not in disabeyance. The magic pentacle can be seen as comprising eight triangles and one pentagon, thus nine forms in ONE and inseparable from the ONE[88]; while the pentagon, so contained, itself contains the pentacle that itself contains eight triangles and a pentagon (nine forms), which, Escher-like, itself contains ... ad infinitum.

Fox's invention of the 9 x 9 formal structure is in keeping with his concept of 'poem as sculpture'[89], a

---

[85] Jan Gullberg, "Mathematics From the Birth of Numbers", "The Nine Point Circle", W W Norton & Co, 1997, page 433.

[86] Maurits Cornelius Escher, 1898-1972, "The Graphic Work", Taschen, 2001.

[87] In a Möbius universe there are only two dimensional worlds that are curved and continuous, in other words continuous and finite, according to Fox. Compare Edwin Abbot Abbot (1838-1926), "Flatland", Princeton University Press (Banchoff, 1991). For detail on Möbius see Jan Gullberg, op cit, page 380.

[88] Jan Gullberg, "Mathematics From the Birth of Numbers", 'Pentacle', W W Norton & Co, 1997, page 420. Also, Dr John Dee and the hexagram.

[89] This is to consolidate T S Eliot's simile of sculpture and its materials being like music's materials in describing how a poet is obliged to work with the sounds he has heard, "The Music of Poetry", 1942.

mentally objective phenomenon (discussed above and in detail elsewhere[90]). However, formality of structure does not mean containment or restriction or constriction of poetic freedom within an out-moded vessel (a poet as mere vassal to form); but that a well founded vessel is capable of carrying an exploring and skilful reader to far flung places of the imagination where the unread[91] easily lose their way and tread in fear. It is startling to note Spenser's own modern, (almost) post-modern[92], view of his own poetic method in "The Faerie Queene" in presenting his distinction between the poetic and the historiographic method of expressing 'knowledge'[93] as in "The Faerie Queene" through the medium of the printed book.

> But, because the beginning of the whole work seemeth abrupte and as depending upon other antecedents, it needs that ye know the occasion of these three knights severall adventures. For the methode of the poet historical is not such, as of an historiographer. For an historiographer discourseth

---

[90] Poem as sculpture is discussed in the introduction to Fox's "Songs of Nocence".

[91] Unread, such as (after Ayto) the Anglo-Saxon King Ethelred II the Unready (ill advised), are those without good counsel, who do not have access or ear for good, knowledgeable advice; a reader being a counsellor, in OE *rede*, unriddler, interpreter, hence someone who could, among other things, read.

[92] What the opaque jargon 'modern', 'post-modern', 'cybennial' is up to is discussed more fully in the introduction to Fox's forthcoming "Songs of Nocence". Essentially they are terms imperfectly identifying kinds of 'perspectivals' that blinker human vision.

[93] Spenser's epistemology must be the subject of major study somewhere, but this editor has not yet found it out. In regard to "utterance", Smith makes the work take on the shape of beaten (*cybennial*) space whereat three forked tongue of tribes curls into being words empty of voices, seeking to vent their meanings upon the breathing air that lives around us.

> of affairs orderly as they were donne, accounting as well the times as the actions; but a poet thrusteth into the middest, even where it most concerneth him, and there recoursing to the things forpaste, and divining of things to come; maketh a pleasing analysis of all.[94]

This is a view taken to heart by Fox's great friend Albert Smith in writing his huge work "utterance of the true thing of it that is"[95].

Smith utterly eschews the current conventions of the medieval word vessel which is the medium of the printed book and has constructed an alternative cybennial form that works for now. Smith is sensitive to the concept reported by Samuel, among others,

> "that the past is plaything of the present, or, as postmodernist theory would have it, a 'metafiction', ...".[96]

Fox's "Queen" has moved away from the postmodernist to the 'post-postmodernist', to the cybennialist era which in an aspect returns to Spenserian times and re-introduces the grand construct, the formal shape, though proportionate to the narrow spans, or short scans, of attention that cybennial psyches operate with. His "Queen" nods towards Samuel's:

> It is arguable that myth, or what F.M. Cornford called 'Mythistoricus' — a history cast in a mould of conception, 'whether artistic or philosophic' which, 'long before the work was contemplated' was already 'inwrought into the very structure of the author's mind' [F.N. Cornford, "Thucydides", p. viii] — is

---

[94] Edmund Spenser, "Letter of the Author's to the right noble and valourous Sir Walter Raleigh, Knight", 23 January 1583. Given by Spenser in introducing "The Faerie Queene".

[95] Albert Smith, "utterance of the true thing of it that is", work in progress, see http://www.justwords.demon.co.uk

[96] Raphael Samuel, "Theatres of Memory", Verso 1994, page 429.

immanent in any historical work. Typically we conflate a great mass of evidence to illustrate or to exemplify relatively simple truths — the classical procedure of the allegorist. Our whole effort is to discover a logic or pattern in seemingly quite fortuitous associations; to give meaning and draw lessons from what might otherwise be a quite random sequence of events. In the terms proposed by Vladimir Propp in his morphology of folk-lore, our narratives conform to 'tale-types'.[97]

But, like Sir Galahad, Fox cannot but continue, in spite of Samuel, his cybennial quest for the mouth of that mythic cauldron wherein the blood of The Word was once gathered and supped in fellowship with meaning, until drained of meaning, leaving only the word, lying among the lees.

There is little doubt in Fox's mind that Spenser's extraordinarily 'modern' outlook in the sixteenth century spilt into his then past through his wonderful 'etymologies' and the massive allegorical extension of "The Faerie Queene" as a whole, and that it acted contemporaneously as an important ingredient in the then (as now) controversial issue of form[98].

---

[97] Raphael Samuel, "Theatres of Memory", Verso, 1994, page 442.

[98] Rosemond Tuve, from "Allegorical Imagery", 1966, in Edmund Spenser, Edited by Paul J Alpers, Penguin, 1969, pages 313-4:
> These oppositions [of structures, *entrelacements* and contra-posing moral figures, or virtues] actually receive most articulate statements in still a different century — Spenser's own. For the modern objections to Spenser's structure are often almost humorously those we hear repeated time and again in the famous quarrel over the structure of Ariosto and later, of Tasso — the structure 'dei romanzi'. It seems to me more likely than not that Spenser's poem, written and published when controversial treatments on one side or the other were coming off the press regularly,

However, in regard to Spenser's 'etymologies', his uses of words, their adoptions and adaptions, they surely pointed his then readers not simply to the past as history, but to the past as 'meaning' now, as in "Time present and time past / Are both per-haps present in time future / And time future contained in time past."[99] Not simply history, but meanings "intermedled"[100], as it were, to fall (accidentally) in the 'now' of it then, and the 'herenow' now.

Yet, even then, in that first Elizabethan age, the potency of Arthurian legend *medled* with the

---

> constitutes a stand taken on the matter — for of course he blithely adopts a 'romance' structure and in the Letter to Raleigh cites as virtues the very disputed characteristics of the accused genre. Conditions of his life perhaps precluded his following all steps of the quarrel, but after warm squabbles in the '50s, it broke out with voluble fervour sustained through the '80s. What we know of Spenser's friends, his interests, and his advocacy of Ariosto in the direct form of declared emulation, disposes us to believe him not naïve about contemporary poetics.

[99] Thomas Stearns Eliot, "Four Quartets", Burnt Norton, 1935, opening lines, The Complete Poems and Plays, Faber & Faber 1969, page 171. I have altered the line very slightly, by introducing the hyphen in 'per-haps"; but this does not, I think, alter meaning more than I intend.

[100] Taken from Spenser's concluding remarks in his letter to Sir Walter Raleigh, op cit. when he excuses or rather explains, somewhat post hoc one feels, the core 'plot' of his Faerie Queene, from which stem the wilderness of offshoots which he describes as:

> But by occasion hereof, many other adventures are intermedled; but rather as accidents than intendments; as the love of Britomart, the overthrow of Marinell, the misery of Florimell, the vertuousness of Belphœbe, the lasciviousness of Hellenora; and many the like.

That he could have reduced the work as a modern screenplay seems certain, though his modern destination would surely have been Hollywood, if not faber & faber.

fertile, perhaps febrile times of the first Elizabeth, to reproduce the ancient fruits of the tree. The conversion of the ancient druidic rites to the Christian celebrations, masses and festivals, (Christmas, Easter[101] etc) remains embedded typically and very influentially in the work of Sir Thomas Malory, who we know died in 1471. Therein we find the Wasteland, a land fallen to waste because of the 'killing of toil' by that, "dolerous stroke [of kynge Hurlaine who clave (killed) kinge Labor]"[102],. And here, and now still, the corpse in "The Wasteland"[103] crops-up again and again in the early 20th century. Across the whole of the span is the vast space intervening between when the mark of the first blood stained the killing stone until the River Thames cleansed the land of a sacrificed child whose torso was consigned to its keeping here and now in 2002[104]. We must surely always have the sacrifice of others in mind.

---

[101] Easter, according to Chambers, comes from the Old English (OE) *Ēastre* meaning 'east', therefore pointing to the pre-Christian Goddess of the Dawn (L *Aurōra* Gk *Ēós*), sunrise.

[102] Edited, Eugène Vinaver, "The Works of Sir Thomas Malory", OUP, 1954, Page 708:
> 'And hit was in the realme of Logris, and so befelle there grete pestilence, and grete harme to bothe reallmys; for there encresed nother corne, ne grasse, nother well-nye no fruyte, ne in the watir was founde no fyssh. Therefore men calle hit — the londys of the two marchys — the Waste Londe, for that dolerous stroke. ...'

[103] Thomas Stearns Eliot, "The Wasteland", 1922, in "The Complete Poems and Plays", Faber & Faber 1969, page 63, lines 71-72:
> 'That corpse you planted last year in your garden, 'Has it begun to sprout?

[104] Reported by the British media in 2002 that an African child had been murdered by sacrifical rite, dismembered alive and disposed in the River Thames, London.

Not only Spenser but Malory is steeped in the ancient and indelible lore of this land of Britain:

> Thes spyndyls [the spindles of the three Fates, one each of white, red and green],' seyde the damesell, 'was whan synfull Eve cam to gadir fruyte, for which Adam and she were put oute of Paradyse. She toke with her the bowgh whych the appyll hynge on, than perseyved she that the braunche was freysh and grene, and she remembird of the losse which cam of the tre. Than she thought to kepe the braunche as long as she myght, and for she had no coffir to kepe hit in, she put hit in the erthe. So by the wylle of oure Lorde the braunche grew to a grete tre within a litill whyle, and was as whyght as ony snowe, braunchis, bowis, and levys: that was a tokyn that a maydyn planted hit. But affter that oure Lorde com to Adam and bade him know hys wyff fleyshly, as nature requyred. So lay Adam with hys wyff undir the same tre, and anone the tre which was whyght felle to grene os ony grasse, and all that com oute of hit. And in the same tyme that they medled togydirs Abell was begotyn.
>
> Thus was the tre longe of grene coloure. And so [hit] befelle many dayes [aftir,] undir the same tre Cayne slew Abell, whereof befelle grete mervayle, for a[s] Abell had ressayved dethe undir the grene tre, he lost the grene coloure and becam rede; that was in tokenyng of blood. And anone all of the plantis dyed thereoff, but the tre grewe and waxed mervaylusly fayre, and hit was the most fayryst tre and the most delectable that ony man myght beholde and se; and so ded the plantes that grewe oute of hit tofore that Abell was slayne undir hit.[105]

---

[105] Edited, Eugène Vinaver, "The Works of Sir Thomas Malory", OUP, 1954, page 711.

In all this 'intermedling' of vegetation with the lifesblood of humanity is the continuance or resurrection of life. And all the while the ancient Greek spindles turn weirdly in the sky and thread their grene and rede and pure white, while the 'tre', a being of indestructible history, stands tall and clear both in its druidic nature and in its etymological reference to the Old English 'Cross'[106], scaffold or Rood in the extraordinary 8th century poem "The Dream of the Rood".

This poem is crucial in representing the metonymic form carrying over from the Pagan to the Christian in the way of making Old English poetry serve the (then) new Christian establishment. This is the 'Cædmon effect' as famously reported by the Venerable Bede[107] in 6th century Northumbria. The

---

[106] 'Tre' cannot but refer to the tree-of-life in all its aspects, from the Druidic through to the Christian, when, by the simplest metonymy, tree stood for the Cross or Rood, the marvelous tree, the brightest wood as in the Old English poem "Dream of the Rood", specifically line 4, Bruce Dickins and Alan S C Ross, "The Dream of the Rood", Methuen Old English Library, 1934-1964, page 20. They give a note on this point, citing the use of "treoth" in the sense of 'cross'. It is Fox's contention that "treoth" is also an OE homophone (a pun) on truth or 'trowe'. It hardly seems possible that Malory, Spenser and the Elizabethan poets generally would not have instinctively carried over the Pagan rites to the Christian which are, in any case, identically primitive in their basic behaviours.

[107] Bede, The Venerable Bede, "The Ecclesiastical History of the English Nation & the Lives of St Cuthbert & the Abbots", translated from the Latin by J Stevens (1723) and others subsequently, Everyman's Library, No 479, Dent, 1910 (1970), page 206-7. Here he describes how Cædmon, a hostler at the monastery, dreamed holy verse. Cædmon was an wholly untaught and unlettered layman who, among other holy verses, dreamt up the now famous and then much admired hymn in OE known as "Cædmon's Hymn". Bede reports that:

> ... a person appeared to him in his sleep, and saluting him by his name, said, "Caedmon, sing some song to me." He answered, "I cannot sing; for that was the reason why I left the entertainment, and retired to this place [the stable] because I could not sing." The other who talked to him, replied, "However, you shall sing."— "What shall I sing?" rejoined he. "Sing the beginning of created beings," said the other. Hereupon he presently began to sing verses to the praise of God, which he had never heard, the purport whereof was thus :— We are now to praise the Maker of the heavenly kingdom, the power of the Creator and his counsel, the deeds of the Father of glory. How He, being the eternal God, became the author of all miracles, who first, as almighty preserver of the human race, created heaven for the sons of men as the roof of the house, and next the earth. This is the sense, but not the words [says Bede] in the order as he sang them in his sleep; for verses, though never so well composed, cannot be literally translated out of one language into another [from the Old English into Latin], without losing much of their beauty and loftiness.

Cædmon's achievement was to 'see' or to be filled with the OE words that could carry over the metaphorical picture of the new monotheistic heaven as a whole using the then new 'Old' English language which until then had contained and expressed only the stories and achievements of the old pagan gods and powers. Cædmon made room for the new One God, the Monarch of the One Realm where mankind could have further life, indeed, eternal life after death, and could live happily in a place just like the Valhalla sky of old, but now taken over by a monopolistic God and rebranded as 'Heaven' whose gate was kept by a monopolistic Church. This 'new' Heaven, though etymologically confused in some degree, is nevertheless found through OE giving 'sky' &/or 'vault' or 'roof'. Cædmon was pointing poetically upwards to that vault, a sky which arches over the earth, and beyond which was the new (re-branded) Valhalla (Brewer's gives 'hall of the slain' for Valhalla). Thus, Cædmon's new poetic versified a vast loft conversion displacing the pagan hall in the sky with the new God's vaster and more impressive Heaven. That 'newness' is 'better' is not just a 20th century fancy after all.

"Tre" here is 'tree-of-life' in all its aspects, from the druidic through to the Christian, when by an extraordinary feat of language the Pagan and the Christian are reconciled through the poetry of the 'tree' standing for the Cross or Rood. It is a simple and powerful metonymy incarnating the idea of Christ's sacrifice on the wooden cross with druidic human sacrifice made to the ancient British oak, the marvelous tree, the brightest wood:

> Hþæt, ic sþefna cyst, secʒan þylle,
> *[what/Lo, I dream best say will,]*
> hwæt mē ʒemætte to midre nihte,
> *[what me dreamt in-to middle night,]*
> sydþan reordberend reste þunedon
> *[thereafter/since people/sons-of-speech rest in/dwell]*
> þuhte me þæt ic ʒesaþe syllicre treoþ

As for the hymn we have the original in various texts, this is from Richard Hamer's 1970 "a choice of Anglo-Saxon Verse", Faber & Faber pages 121-123, with Fox's literal translation interlaced:

> Nū scylun hergan hefænrīcæs Uard,
> *[Now shall/must praise/extol heaven's reich/domain/watch/guard]*
> Metudæs mæcti end His mōdgidanc,
> *[Maker god/creator mighty and his purposeful mind]*
> uerc Uuldurfadur, suē Hē uundra gihuæs,
> *[work wonder father began he wonder all]*
> ēci Dryctin, ōr āstelidæ.
> *[everlasting leader origin started/established]*
> Hē ǽrist scōp ælda barnum
> *[He first shaped (our) elders' children]*
> heben til hrōfe, hāleg Scepen.
> *[heaven as roof whole/holy made]*
> Thā middungeard moncynnæs Uard,
> *[Then world-earth/middle-earth mankind guarder]*
> ēci Dryctin, æfter tīadæ
> *[eternal Leader after adorned/ordained]*
> firum foldu, Frēa allmectig.
> *[men/life earth/field Lord all mighty/sword.]*

> *[Thought me that I saw   marvelous/bright*
> *tree/truth/cross]*[108]

The Cross is seen as the tree of truth upon which the bloodlife of the King of kings was sacrificed in druidic groves where boughs of mistletoe sprang green and white from the winter oaks after their golden summer. Thus, the tree cannot but remain the core image of the British peoples and the bright light of it, the "syllicre treoþ" like the sun, bringing ever continuing life to them.

Although not a natural monarchist, Fox is certainly opposed to the idea of yet another politician occupying palatial British offices jammed with cronies and the cronies of cronies on large salaries absorbing well hidden benefits, unusual expenses and wielding disproportionate influence. He imagines yet another poorly turned out election for a badly proportioned President selected from a party list, or worse, a massive turnout to choose between a known crook and a Nazi[109]. Fox has a fearful sense of that other fairy story[110] in which an Orwellian Napoleon sits smiling in the wings mouthing "Beasts of England". His clear preference is for a known, more or less controllable institution the head of which is accidentally appointed from time to time, as some would say by 'God'. As a

---

[108] "The Dream of the Rood", op cit, lines 1-4, with Fox's 'literal' translation interlaced.

[109] See French Presidential election 2002, Chirac or La Pen.

[110] George Orwell, "Animal Farm: A Fairy Story", 1945. The chapter one anthem of that wise old pig Major "Beasts of England" finishes with the golden lines of ultimate irony when sung at Manor Farm when man and pig have transmogrified, becoming indistinguishable one from the other, and Major's prophetic skull is well, if not truly, buried:
> Beasts of England, beasts of Ireland,
> Beasts of every land and clime,
> Hearken well and spread my tidings
> Of the golden future time.

believing atheist, Fox would not say 'god', but speak of the less divinely authoritative, though still mysterious, 'chance'[111]. If such a process results in a bad egg being

---

[111] In this he is more afraid of the son, Prince Charles, than his mother with her anointed, unilateral commitment to the perpetual defence of the monolithic Church of England, incidentally perpetuating the inherent historical divisions among British Christians, and Christians world wide. For the monarch to become defender of Faith at large is, of course, a much greater threat to atheists, agnostics, humanists and secularists, than to the Church of England and its perks and privileges. Fox would not wish to associate the Dionysians or such modern 'mediaevil' 'big brotherish indulgers' with the purity of Atheism. His instinct is to exclude, in my view wrongly, sects in pursuit of happiness through peculiar gratifications of their senses through consumption of the subservient &/or the defeated. Or those sects merely committed to the ingesting of food, drink, music, headstuffs, salves, sex, endless clubbing, the consumption of blood and flesh, the manifold fluid pleasures of the religious imbibing salvation through the various orifices of man and beast. By excluding such atavistic originals still taking their pleasures of the grove, Fox is mis-analysing the 'nature' of their behaviour. Fox and I disagree on this point, he being a puritanical Atheist, while I am a somewhat lower case 'catholic' atheist.

However, Prince Charles' move, while doubtless perfectly sincere in itself, is effectively a very astute political adjustment that will secure the (psephological) position of the future King as the 'chosen' of the tribe, it being in the interests of a much wider range of sectional religious interests to support the Crown, not as embodying their religious leadership, but as protector of their interests to extend and perpetuate themselves. Ultimately such a move is likely to ensure defeat of any threat to the crown by further republican onslaughts engineered by media moguls such as Rupert Murdock whose peculiar hatred of the British has been particularly eroding. His cunning exploitation of the age old process of appointing lapdog editors and commentators to snarl and sniff at the central, defining institution of the British, the constitutional Monarchy, has been wounding and wearing, but not fatal; like constant

crowned then the British have ways of getting that egg to fall, as of old, even if some sacrifice is required to get the right head in the crown.

More important than the mere psephology of the matter is Fox's sensing of a primitive need for a person to be above the mere anarchic mass, the tribe in tribulation, the people as children in need of a powerful parent. Thus, his "Fairy Queen" is a poem that literally incorporates the long trail back to pre-historic rites that persist today beneath the grand forms and foibles of modern royal ceremonial supposedly invented by the Victorians (what didn't they invent?). In the "Fairy Queen" Fox is illuminating the nature of 'kinship' and the quasi-elective process that produces a crown in which a head is tolerated providing it can bear the tribal need for human sacrifice which remains at the core of the British psyche.

Fox, among other things, is asking the reader to make the salutary comparison between the staggering advances of the 16th Century Elizabethans

---

pruning perhaps it has created fresh growth. As has his promotion &/or protection of certain British politicians, strangely not conservatives (the certain monarchists), but New Labour whereof republican influence might still be found lurking in the dim recesses of constituency branch rooms.

Nevertheless, Prince Charles' 'Faith' (& RESPECT) move is undoubtedly astute and also a way of reducing social conflict. His Father's essay on conflict, in "A Question of Balance", 1982, is interesting in this regard and perhaps has been influential on Charles— see below. In the end, Fox's only defence against such charitable 'initiatives' would be to rely on the fact that atheism is ultimately a 'belief', in other words a 'faith' in lower case, and, therefore, surely eligible for lottery grants and other such 'funny money' subsidies readily available in Britain as stealth support to such as the inculcators of yet more superstitions in children by extending the privileges of so called 'special' schools. This is discussed in more depth in the introduction to "Songs of Nocence".

and their adventures and fights to achieve self-gratification, with the staggering decline of the 20th Century Elizabethans who achieve self-gratification by anxiously sucking at the great tit of popular consumption. Thus, we find the threefold structure of Fox's "Fairy Queen": the surface 'personal' humanity of the woman at the heart of the Jubilee event (the celebrant, the day-off in the Sun, & other modern mediaevilisms[112]); the Spenserian comparison with the enchanted, magical, Fairy Queen; and the atavistic character of the golden bough presiding over chalice and cauldron[113] in which the blood of mistletoe with the juice of maidens and men is squeezed and supped with their blood whilst warm beneath oaks, hearts opened to

---

[112] 'Mediaevil', this is not a misspelling of medieval, but an inkhorn term invented by Fox to describe the parallel between the state of present day media, with its Barons and Princes, being much akin to the medieval church in Europe as we know from Chaucer, 1343-1400; being comprised, as now, of a Pope plus the Princes of the Church supported by a vast and largely useless bureaucracy that controlled communications in society. Not to mention a very motley of Friars, Summoners and Pardoners at home in the ale house, "in the devil's church". In other words, for those of who don't know Chaucer, the corrupt, the overbearing, the pious, the perverted, the unscrupulous etc; a body of institutionalised perversion, a vast, crawling, bloated parasite hunched on the backs of the peasants and artisans doing all the work. So, what's new?

[113] Cauldron, the most famous and magnificent example of a prehistoric cauldron ever found is the "Gundestrup Cauldron", beautifully photographed centrefold (pages 67-70), in Lionel Casson, "The Barbarian Kings", Select Books, Tree Communications Inc., New York, Great Britain, 1983:

> Caldrons were sacred vessels to the Celts. At rites Druids filled them with potions made from mistletoe and other plants believed to give health and fertility. At sacrifices caldrons caught the blood of human victims, and the Celts also regarded them as symbols of plenty.

their gods[114]. Here lies the great cauldron, the chalice of truth wherein the blood of Christ was first drained from his living flesh and drunk to libate his sweet and tender, to wash his heavenly flesh through the tooth and tongue and into the belly of earthly peoples.

---

[114] Timothy Taylor, "The Prehistory of Sex", Fourth Estate, London, 1996, page 215. Taylor observes, in regard to the Gundestrup Cauldron, that of the various figures depicted on the silver plaques that fit all round the hemispheric bowl:
> The most striking seems at first to be sitting in a cross-legged pose, eyes in a trance, wearing a stag antlered cap and holding a neck ring [torus] in his/her right hand. A rather phallic ram-headed snake is in the left hand, and the figure—often identified as the Celtic God Cernunnos—is surrounded by animals. The figure is of indeterminate sex, with neither breasts nor beard. What is most important is the pose. The legs are not actually on the ground but are raised up. Although it is hard to see it at first, the whole figure is levitated on one toe. (The ground line is clearly defined by the adjacent stag's hooves.) The right heel is sandwiched between the left thigh and the crotch, so as to put pressure directly on the perineum—the point between the scrotum and anus. The figure has been depicted in one of the advanced positions (*asanas*) of Tantric Yoga, a type of yoga that varies from the more recent ascetic tradition in that it focuses on animal energies. Those who practise it may use both sex and drugs in order to reach altered states of consciousness.

This certainly bears out Ward Rutherford's 1978 conclusion that we can attribute to the Druids such skills as:
> Taking all things into consideration, one might conclude that what has been lost was less an ancient wisdom, than what we might call "an Ancient Skill", an ability to harness the forces of the mind. Of this we have some inkling in the great Yogi and Fakirs of Hinduism whose amazing abilities are only now[,] and very tentatively at that, being taken seriously.

This is taken from "The Druids: Magicians of the West", The Aquarian Press, 1978, page 171.

These references are to the pagan origins of the British monarchy[115] and their continuing inherence in the national psyche and indeed in the natural psyches of all peoples of the earth[116]. The need for parentage with supernatural, superhuman, magical powers of protection was and is lodged deep in all humankind. The role of the ruler, the Royal-Being, the special being, the magical figure, is well known to be of fundamental importance in serving this need. Jessie Weston observed:

> We have found, further, that this close relation between the ruler and his land, which resulted in the ill of one becoming the calamity of all, is no mere literary invention, proceeding from the fertile imagination of a twelfth century court poet, but a deeply rooted popular belief, of practically immemorial antiquity and inexhaustible vitality; we can trace it back thousands of years before the Christian era, we find it fraught with decisions of life and death today.[117]

From then through to here and now is only a very short step, though it seems endlessly riddled with recurrence of images, of small gods that insist on surviving, who weirdly resurrect time and again their truth trees, their oaks, their mistletoe, holly, laurel and crosses, sun, stones, the white and the green and the red threads, mysteriously spindled.

Such is the weaving of the fates of knights errant medled of damsels, their laying waste maidens

---

[115] William A Chaney, "The Cult of Kingship in Anglo-Saxon England: The Transition From Paganism To Christianity", Manchester University Press, 1970 [1999], specifically page 108 (Chapter III, "The Sacrificial King").
[116] This is exemplified in the continuing (inexplicable) existence (persistence) of the Commonwealth with the Queen as its Head in title and in practice.
[117] Jessie L Weston, "From Ritual to Romance", [CUP, 1920], Anchor Books, 1957, page 65 (chapter VI "The Symbols").

and lands in error. The interlacing of all such travail through intervening minds and mentalities whereof all their cunning, liquid threads twist all that has and will ensue of the unbroken passions of being alive and here, and needing, insisting on, incarnation in the living form of a royal person. A desiderative form in gold incarnate to cover our need for reality, for a golden life married to that golden bough that grows, an ineluctable tongue of gold, from the mouth of the tree that waits for the sun to bring its rites over death ever forth, again and again. Here the human person is incarnated by wordless acts that gleam but cannot be transcribed. Here the recurring images are the icons of the poet who sees himself bathed in sunlight incarnate.

> One day, nigh wearie of the yrkesome way,
> From her unhastie beast she did alight;
> And on the grasse her dainty limbs did lay
> In secrete shadow, far from all mens sight;
> From her fayre head her fillet she undight,
> And layd her stole aside: Her angels face,
> As the great eye of heaven, shyned bright,
> And made a sunshine in the shady place;
> Did never mortall eye behold such heavenly grace.[118]

The Royal-Being thus 'elected', the chosen one, is responsible for the good and ills that follow.

To a degree this does still refer to Queen Elizabeth II's selection in virtue of her Uncle's rejection (abdication[119]). Admittedly, this is to some extent 'democratic', which can be recognised in the 'kin(g)ship' issue of 'electing' a new King from leading kin by the elders of the tribe when the old kin(g) had died. However, this would be to presume that selection thus was to do with some kind of fairness idea. It would

---

[118] Edmund Spenser, "The Faerie Queene", Book I, Canto III, stanza 4.
[119] Edward VIII's abdication can hardly be described as voluntary.

seem that this is a presumption too far. It is much more likely that the 'democratic' process was to choose the most suitable being to fulfill the role envisaged, and such a role did, and does, include its sacrificial dimension[120]. There is a clean difference between a sovereign and subjects according to England's Charles I in 1649. Nothing could rise above a sovereign but a divine rite of the people.

> At the King's sign that he was ready, the executioner raised the axe and severed the head at one blow. A great groan went up from the crowd, which was immediately cleared from the street by the troopers.[121]

---

[120] William A Chaney, op cit, pages 17-18.
[121] On the beheading of King Charles I, D R Watson, "The Life and Times of Charles I", Weidenfeld and Nicolson, 1972, page 188.

Commentary

Stanza 1

The poem opens with direct reference to Fox going, on the morning of Thursday 2nd May 2002, to the City of Bath, England, finding a viewing position near the Guildhall behind the temporary crowd control railings in The High Street. After waiting an age, and gradually being eased to the back by ruthless women and children, he managed to actually peer punningly at his Queen walking down the High Street to the Abbey. There she was, of a sudden, under the watchful eye of Special Branch and sharpshooters positioned on the Abbey roof, among a general scuffle of Ladies-in-Waiting, Dignitaries, Officials, youthful Cadets of the Armed Forces, Security Officers, Police and Traffic Wardens. It was the first time he had seen her in the flesh. Of course, he had chosen the wrong side of the street to wait for her and had to be content with a hand from the good old Duke, who always covers the wrong side on walkabouts, presenting himself as the consolation prize.

The stanza has a simple narrative style, a face in the crowd, a man-in-the-street approach to the Queen, the common intimacy of the first person plural ("we"). However, the first line deliberately echoes T S Eliot's "Journey of the Magi"[122], and has perhaps other resonances. It also refers to the simple fact that if you want to see the Queen it is hard work, you do need to

---

[122] Thomas Stearns Eliot, "Journey of the Magi"[the three wise men], Ariel Poems, The Complete Poems and Plays, Faber and Faber, 1969, page 103, lines 16-20:

> A hard time we had of it.
> At the end we preferred to travel all night,
> Sleeping in snatches,
> With the voices singing in our ears, saying
> That this was all folly.

rise early, or stay up all night, to secure your place; you need to be patient, diplomatic, yet determined and ruthless, as in life generally, about keeping your place once you have secured one. The "we" is the crowd in general, but it also refers to Fox's immediate companion, his friend and lover Khun Siriluck, a Thai lady whose own long serving monarch, the genuinely kind and supremely able King Bhumibol Adulyadej[123], has ensured she is, like most Thais, an extremely committed monarchist.

Seeing her "for real" introduces a golden[124] thread as well as a strand of Fox's philosophical

---

[123] King of Thailand, 1946 to date. Although not crowned until seven days after his marriage to Queen Sirikit on 28th April 1950, he acceded on 9th June 1946. In this he has technically reigned for nearly sixty years, and is therefore the longest reigning constitutional monarch in the world, even if dating from his coronation in 1950. There is no doubt at all that he is sincerely and deeply loved by the Thai people virtually without exception, not simply because of the powerful Thai tradition of respect for royalty, but also because he is now a very senior person by virtue of his age and in virtue of his manifest devotion to his coronation oath: "We will reign with righteousness for the benefit of the Siamese people". In this there is a remarkable similarity between the two oldest serving and most significant monarchs in the world. The old name for Thailand was Siam, changed by Proclamation 11th May 1949, to "Prathet Thai" which means "Land of the Free", hence Thailand.

[124] Real is an etymological pun on gold, which also carries the image of the sun and of the mistletoe as it transforms through the golden Autumn to renew its pure white fruits and pure green boughs. Robert Graves is interesting on 'real' in his amusing "Oxford Addresses on Poetry", Cassell, 1961, in "Poetic Gold", page 88, addressed to the Philological Society:

> I held it up [the (supposedly) solid gold medal of the Prince Alexander Droutzkoy Memorial Award], and began discoursing on gold, the royal metal, the only one found in a pure state, a metaphor for truth and integrity and, because royal and real are the same

concern with the age old issue of appearance and reality. The intensely personal "And there I was [cæsura[125]] lost in the forest of faces" recalls the Spenserian foliage and the primitive forest, as well as

---

> word, for reality. To be paid in gold is to be paid *really*: not in promissory notes or base metal. 'The testing or assaying of doubtful gold,' I went on, 'has given numerous words to the English language—"touchstone", "acid test", and even the word *test* itself. The original noun "test" meant the cupel in which refiners parted gold from other metals; hence the phrase "put it to the test".' Hence also the phrase used by the Earl of Montrose in speaking of love:
>
>> He either fears his fate too much,
>> Or his deserts are small,
>> Who dares not put it to the touch
>> To gain or lose it all.

Well, I couldn't resist making this an overlong quotation so that I could include Graves' lovely Montrose (1612-50) quote though it doesn't have much to do with Fox's "Queen"; a nice touch.

Such typical concern with gold and its purity is in Gabriel Harvey's correspondence with Edmund Spenser (M *Immerito* — the undeserving) when distinguishing the work of "Mr Sidney and M Dyer the two very Diamondes of hir Maiesties Courte for many speciall and rare qualities, as to helpe forwarde our new famous enterprise for the Exchanging of Barbarous and Balductum Rymes with Artificiall Verses, the one being in manner of pure and fine Goulde, the other but counterfeit and base ylfauoured Copper." — from "Elizabethan Critical Essays", edited G Gregory Smith, OUP, 1904, volume 1, page 101.

[125] The cæsura is not marked with a comma because Fox dislikes in principle the use of punctuation marks in poetry. He holds that all punctuation is almost entirely redundant in poetry because the poetic diction, the syntax of the poetry itself is perfectly sufficient to ensure understanding without the archaic limits, constraints and confusions introduced by punctuation. He has retained the full stop closing each stanza to signify that they are not intended to 'run' into each other as such, but to stand distinct like Spenserian stanzas.

his literal surprise at finding himself as one of a crowd, participating strangely in the apparently mundane. The narrative begins to compress the actual into an image of the intimate distance between the Queen and the almost hidden people of the royal forest. Fox is "there", not 'here', thus introducing an ecstatic distance between himself as participant, and him as observer.

The strength of the norms, the traditions that rule the forest are exemplified by the steel of the rails and the almost involuntary nature of the 'places' for which people have pressed. The precise meanings and characters of the etymologies of 'fence', 'rail', 'steel' and the lively, electrifying meaning of 'galvanised', all contribute to the just and balanced compression of a 'history' of both the moment and of the monarchy itself into just a couple of lines. The precise use of the word 'person' (L. persōna — mask) in this regard is critical to Fox's unveiling procedure and characteristic of his approach to the construction of poetic machinery as precision instrument.

Fox's use of rhyme is not merely to "set off wretched and lame meeter" as Milton famously argued[126], but operates with precision to draw words together. For example, three key words in regard to the Queen's personality, bbb, "real" with "steel" with "feel". Thus, we should take Fox's precise use of rhyme in conjunction with his use of the literal to dramatise and renew the commonplace. For example, with the literally exact "A person you could almost feel", "so close she seemed and clear", Fox creates a dramatic resolution of tension between the need and the reality. He also exploits the etymological ambiguity in 'close'[127]

---

[126] John Milton, "Paradise Lost", Preface to the 1669 edition.
[127] We have Ayto, Skeat and Chambers for this, giving Old French *clos* through *clore* 'shut' (related to L *clāvis* 'key') all through to the English of embracement, such as: clause, clavier, clef, cloister, closet, clove, conclave, conclude, enclave,

that derives from 'to close (as a door)' and 'to bring together'. Fox has always at his back that sad example of rhyme (and metre) dictating poor Rupert Brooke's poem "The Old Vicarage, Grantchester", right down to its last couplet when we are stuck with tea at ten to three for all eternity, rather than at four[128].

---

include, preclude. Such English expresses the embraced, the 'included'; but paradoxically, as Fox intends, such 'inclusiveness' necessarily implies its contrary 'exclusiveness'.
[128] Rupert Brooke, 1887-1915, "Rupert Brooke: Collected Poems", with a memoir by Edward Marsh, London July 1918, Sidgwick & Jackson, third Edition, 1942:
> Deep meadows yet, for to forget
> The lies, and truths, and pain? ... oh! yet
> Stands the Church clock at ten to three?
> And is there honey still for tea?

Here Brooke is so awfully memorable. By 1942 Sidgwick and Jackson had reached 31 impressions in four editions, and the lines had been anthologised and quoted *in extremis*. This was pop poetry still in full swing though Brooke died, on active service though not in action, of dysentery at 4.46 pm on Friday 23rd April 1915. He was buried the same evening on the Greek Island of Scyros. Most striking is that Rupert Brooke's death seems almost the last death of those times when there was time to give it the consideration and expression of loss and grief of friends, for **all** his fellow officers who had mourned his death so expressively and sincerely were themselves to die prematurely in the appalling wave of killing that followed within six weeks at Gallipoli, or a little later on the Western Front, see civ, op cit. Brooke, of course, is most commonly remembered for the opening lines of perhaps his last poem (page 150, op cit) "The Soldier":
> If I should die, think only this of me:
> That there's some corner of a foreign field
> That is forever England. ...

The whole poem is disregarded nowadays as being overly sentimental and shallow, but Fox and I love it as a perfectly genuine expression of an atheistic, young humanist's ideal of 'goodness', in spite of the now politically incorrect last line where we find peace unexhumed, but "under an English heaven". We imagine all the vast acreages of committees, councils and the usual array of equal opportunities

This opening stanza brings the Queen into immediate focus as one 'event' in an ordinary life, lost in the forest. It begs the question as to why this should be so, why is it that someone like Fox, a natural sceptic, and his companion of an entirely non-British culture, and all the other denizens of that forest, should be so affected by this curiously mundane event, of someone walking by, of someone appearing, on the face of it, just like anyone's Mum or Grandma?

Stanza 2

Here the event is recounted in the simplest of terms, but through the presence not of the Queen herself who is lost among a crowd of her own, but the sudden apparent disorder (flurry[129]) of retinue passing

---

opportunists having a field day excising Brooke's poetic grave of all reference to such an heaven (ignoring the poetical correctness of the OE etymology of *heofon*).

[129] On my questioning the choice of this word, Fox's response was that he had had a complex set of issues to consider and had considered them at length before deciding on "flurry'. He explained that in creating the line he had, in simple terms, eventually reduced the choice to 'stir' or "flurry" (this word being the central action of the stanza though it seems focused on the Duke). He had been attracted, and still is, to using 'stir' because it is direct and its etymological thrust relatively clear and strong. The etymological issue was between 'stir' as given by Ayto, Chambers, Skeat, as OE *styrian* 'to move, stir', then through to Old High German *stóren* 'to scatter destroy'. Whereas, "flurry", (not given by Ayto) but according Chambers and specifically Skeat, we find (Scandinavian) 'hurry' through to Swedish *flurig* 'disordered dissolute', and to *flur* 'disordered hair, whim', giving an appropriate lightness to the word. Thus, in the end, he felt the etymological thrust of 'stir' was too strong and off-balanced the stanza as a whole. Additionally, he liked "flurry" because it is disyllabic and in vocalising the line it forces a stretch on the reciter, ensuring the pure sound, the 'air', of the word hangs as it expresses at the point, becoming an onomatopœia of the action it

by. Being on the wrong side, Fox shook hands with the old Duke of Edinburgh. Someone he is very fond of, a character generally caricatured as a narrow, crusty, right wing, crypto-fascist[130] by cheapskate sub-editors

---

describes. This seems convincing enough to me, a mere editor, pleased to have been spared the full explanation.
[130] That such a caricature is plainly unjust and destructive can be readily understood by simple reference to his 1982 book, "A Question of Balance", Michael Russell (Publishing Ltd). For example (Chapter I, "On Conflict", pages 15-16):
> Compare Karl Marx's life story with that of Jesus Christ. Disregarding for a moment the divine element, I think it would be fair to say that Jesus was born apparently out of wedlock to a temporarily homeless artisan. He narrowly escaped political murder as a baby and was brought up as a carpenter who spent his life preaching love and forgiveness. Eventually this man was arrested, tortured and tried in secret — against Jewish law — for preaching that God is love. He was condemned to a criminal's death. Perhaps most astonishing of all is that He left nothing in writing. In modern terms He might be described as an underprivileged, colonial, working class victim of political and religious persecution. Yet He only sought to influence men in their behaviour towards each other through their belief in God and promised paradise in the next world, whereas the middle-class intellectual [Marx] sought absolute political power and expected to achieve paradise in this world.
>
> It is a further irony that the man who institutionalised class-warfare and glorified totalitarianism should have lived out his life in the safety of a tolerant and peaceful democratic society, while the man who worked so hard to heal divisions and reconcile enemies should have met such a violent end in what was virtually a theocratic state.

Naturally, if any journalist troubled to read the Duke then we would surely receive the headline "Jesus Christ a Bastard, says Duke"; no matter that it is obvious to anyone that his views, though moderately and unsurprisingly conservative, are those of a thoughtful, intelligent, fair minded person of his age.

Of course, we have the infamous "slitty eyed" headlines; yet any serious analysis would show that 'slitty eyed' translated into Chinese would seem perfectly okay to any of the billions of people with slitty eyes there and elsewhere. Indeed, it is surely a matter of concern that the racist slant given to this was assuredly in the twisted eye of some reporters, those who saw slitty eyes as being such an awful mongoloid characteristic it dared not be mentioned. Fox, with his long and intimate experience of the East, finds it astonishing that the British media should have had the gross insensitivity to tell people it was bad thing to have slitty eyes, that it was so bad to have slitty eyes that it was a scandalous insult even to refer to such in jest. In fact, the insulting was done not by the joking Duke, but by those ever pious lapdogs making such a gratuitously crass interpretation. Naturally, once the mob is told that 'slitty' is insulting then the 'popular democracy' of meaning seems to take over. This is on a par with the grotesque distortion, made on the Today programme (UK BBC Radio 4) and elsewhere, when some years ago the news entertainer 'Humpy' twisted the use of 'Mongol' as applied to people with the Down's Syndrome handicap. This kind of cheapskate news entertainment takes no account of the fact that the larger part of the world's population is gifted with mongoloid features. That such people might find it problematic to see their features presented as typical of the mentally and physically handicapped did not seem a matter of concern to the 'Humpy' mentality. Yet, it is (or was) an accurate description of the typical features of those wonderful *othergifted* people which should surely have been considered a term of endearment and respect and not an insult to both those billions of the East, or those *othergifted,* with Down's Syndrome, who are not aborted after pre-natal diagnosis. Equally, the political correctness that attempted to define all non-whites as black, although so many of the world's people are brown and yellow, is simply an obscenity. To say this person is yellow or this black or another brown seems straightforwardly unbiased enough, although, of course, almost always inaccurate. As is the attempt to label people by their ethnic origins so as to slot them as readily manipulable data into the latest lump of software designed to

intent on getting easy byelines to impress their lapdog editors.

However, the Old Duke emerges in Fox's "Queen" as a significant and influential figure "behind the throne", with side reference to the 'firm'[131] with its etymology taking us back to the problem of the family name. That someone of the Duke's substantial and independent personality, who, in his time "sailed free and easy", should have kept in step, and one step behind his wife, can only be explained in the light of a 'deal' done just between the two of them beyond the ambit of the courtiers controlling her office and his.

Fox incorporates the Duke's role and history as Prince Consort in the poem by reference to the Duke's early experience as an unknown naval officer with a 'future' in the Royal Navy, whose thoughts and opinions were once of no more interest to anyone than those of his friends and fellow officers, until catapulted from the deck of his ship into the arms of the press when his every word was shot down, caught, weighed, salted and sold by the pound. Nothing about Elizabeth II can be complete without careful consideration of the key role of her third cousin Lieutenant Philip Mountbatten RN, who saw active service in World War

---

produce an 'analysis' that is a weapon to demonstrate why someone owes someone else something for nothing. Such statistical clap-trap is for politicians and that vast, dreary army of petty nonentities infesting smart offices and building lucrative careers on the infections of dissent.

[131] 'Firm: apart from this being a nickname for the royal family itself, and meaning simply 'stable, strong, immovable', it also goes back, according to Ayto among others, through L. *firmus*, to confirm *firma* signature, and by extension to the 'name under which the business is carried out'; it is also related to 'farm', 'firmament', 'furl'.

II, a Prince of Greece, great grandson of Queen Victoria and, it turns out, always a British citizen[132].

In this Fox again pursues the etymological to encompass the nature of the Duke's experience. Each word unravels precisely, only to be woven again to form a web, a net, of meanings that catch the Duke's predicament. Of course, nautical terms prevail even to the shallows, the shoals[133], where he had floundered, fraught, weighed with too much thought, though his words were blown and his 'groans'[134] were grinned open mouthed across the fleet, but not the fleet he knew and loved.

Stanza 3

Again, Fox's concern with Philip, and recognition of his importance to the Queen and to the constitutional monarchy, is carried through the stanza until he places him stranded like Canute[135] standing

---

[132] It was later determined that Philip was not in fact in need of naturalisation in 1946, because its was found, in 1972, that he had been British at birth under a 1705 Act of Parliament that made all descendants of Princess Sophie of Hanover British subjects.

[133] 'Shoals', this pun is given by Ayto as, 'shallows', and 'schools' both of fish and of the schooling of children.

[134] Ayto tells us that: groan and grin are from the same root. He says, "... prehistoric Indo-European *ghrei-*, which seems to have meant something like 'be open'. It has been suggested as the source of a range of verbs which started off denoting simply 'open the mouth', but have since differentiated along the lines 'make noise' and 'grimace'. *Grin* has taken the latter course, but close relatives, such as Old High German *grennan* 'mutter' and Old Norse *grenja* 'howl', show that the parting of the semantic ways was not so distant in time. OE *grennian* actually meant 'draw back the lips and bare the teeth in pain or anger'. — *Groan* [OE], on the other hand, is firmly in the 'make noise' camp".

[135] King Cnut the Great, (Knut Sveinsson) King of England 1016, and of Denmark 1018, and of Norway 1030, died 1035. The tradition has somehow become established that this

against the tide. This, at once romantic, yet absurd image, is intended to beg the question as to why Canute, a seaman of the first rank, should be caricatured as doing something so palpably daft as to try and hold back the tide[136]. Again the nautical vocabulary prevails as Philip's career is washed away, wrecked, ending up yet another naval officer on the beach, once a man of what was then still, and is yet, Nelson's navy, not even a figurehead, yet in a position on board to rock the boat disastrously.

The imagery and decisive ambiguities become suddenly intense and passionate in this stanza. His words like fish flashing as they break surface and fly free, are netted[137] in the air and landed ... . Fox is merciless with the incisive puns on 'twist', 'lie', 'rot', 'fare' and the developing imagery of the beach and the breach and iteration of "pressed", "waded in", and the impossibility of holding back time and change, being "high and dry", "floundered".

It is this 'schooling' of Philip Mountbatten in his role as mere consort that dominates the stanza, only to be overtaken by the flood tide of change that

---

extraordinarily effective ruler of the seagoing was so unwise that he demonstrated his folly by trying to hold back the tide. This is, of course, pure nonsense, presumably invented by some Old English newsworder ingratiating himself with another dynastic house. It is certain that Cnut was demonstrating that there were realistic limits of his powers as King, that the tide was in God's hands, not his, that his people's expectations of him were becoming, perhaps, somewhat unrealistic.

[136] Tide refers to the tide of change that has washed Britain hither over the fifty years. Ayto says etymologically 'tide' [OE] originally meant 'time', and is often used tautologically as 'time and tide wait for no man'. And 'tide' ultimately goes back to the Indo-European base *di* which meant 'divide, cut up', to mean a period or portion of time.

[137] Thus, for example, netted and networked.

rushes upon the monarchy through the last years of the 20th century with the "troublesome sea" of stanza 4.

Stanza 4

The sea image carries us into this stanza. We are washed through by its currents and cross tides into the undertows of the ambiguities, the cross talk of its diction. In this, the stanza needs no Shakespeare, no need for that degree in English literature, it is enough to apply the untrammeled mind simply to the words and their relations. Thereof the stanza's storyline is about cleanness, pure soap washing through the grubby fabric of a society all at sea without a ship, lost happily in a damp mist of its own making.

But if we have a Shakespearean bent, then we find we are also awash with the contrasting images of the bloody and murderous "tragedies" and of the enchanting and magical "Tempest". The image of Hamlet and the royal tragedies, the deadly family intrigues for the crown, and the image of the lovely, romantic Miranda and Ferdinand are intense contrasts, representing the extremes of the royal (real) life and death of Kings and Queens.

The Shakespearean sea change metaphor is itself washed, or sloshed through to modern times where the old style Elizabethan "Tempest", wrought by enchantments, now wreaks havoc with the ideas woven in the worn fabric of a society that had been made in that very Shakespearean age when empire was being built by brutally ruling the waves. Such "troublesome seas", carrying even yet the baffled thoughts and feelings of Prince Philip, wreak[138], drive meanings out

---

[138] Wreak' according to Ayto comes from OE *wreak* or Germananic *wrecan* meaning 'drive out'; Skeat and Chambers include a strong reference to OE *wrecan* meaning 'vengeance'. We have the effect of a cluster 'to drive out', 'to exile', 'to punish', 'to revenge', 'to damage'.

from the multiple ambiguity of "old Britannia[139] turned to scrap", to flood the minds of attentive readers with the nature and irretrievability of a lost past.

Thought of Shakespeare, of Hamlet locked in the castle of his own personality, and the trap of Prospero's Island[140], connects the three ages of Elizabeth: her youthful, unburdened days as the pretty Princess, her latter days now as a golden Jubilee Queen, and also the first age of her namesake Elizabeth I[141].

The extraordinary Shakespearean Elizabethan image of the sea is reduced to the absurd as it "froths

---

[139] This refers to the parallel between the expedient scrapping of the Royal Yacht Britannia for political reasons, and the decline of the British Empire, Britannia ruled the waves.

[140] Prospero's Island, is a reference to Shakespeare himself, who is likely to have been the magician on the Island of his own invention, the star of "The Tempest", 1611 (Rowse, 1978). Prospero is a much discussed Shakespearean persona and has even been likened to Nietzsche's superman (Öberman) by G Wilson Knight, OUP, 1946. Yet, Fox certainly intends to bring Hamlet, 1601 (Rowse, 1978), also to mind, whose "sea of troubles" describe the realities of the throne with cruel precision. Thus, we have the romantic ideal of the enchanted couple in Miranda and Ferdinand protected by the magic of a great Dee-like Magus, Prospero, her Father, in contrast with the murderous realities of Hamlet's predicament wherein there is no limit in the struggle for ultimate power. On the one hand the wand of magic, while in the other, the unused dagger, then the poisoned chalice, the drinking of hot blood and the prick of the poisoned sword.

[141] In considering the importance of Prince Philip, the old Duke, we need not look beyond Elizabeth I and her dangerous relationship with the overweening Robert Dudley, Earl of Leicester, and her eventual death as a spinster with no issue. For Princess Lilibet to have found a loving, but less dangerous, companion through the years of her reign is surely an inestimable boon.

and foams"[142] around the "mother of the free"[143] in her kitchen, the female stereotypical victim among the soap

---

[142] Foam is a material entity referred to in an Indian legend parallel to the Balder myth of the northern regions. Fraser reports it in the Golden Bough thus:
> ... Indra swore to the demon Namuci that he would slay him neither by day nor night, neither with staff nor with bow, neither with the palm of the hand nor with the fist, neither with the wet nor with the dry. But he killed him in the morning twilight by sprinkling over him the foam of the sea. The foam of the sea is just such an object as a savage might choose to put his life in, because it occupies that sort of intermediate or nondescript position between earth and sky or sea and sky in which primitive man sees safety.

Op cit, page 206. It may also reference to Kurma, Amrita, Ambrosia, the food for the immortals churned from the ocean, see Chambers, and "A Dictionary of Non-Christian Religions", Geoffrey Parrinder, Hulton, 1971, 1981.

[143] From the first line in the 'second national anthem' drawn from Sir Edward Elgar's beautiful 1901 "Pomp and Circumstance" march number one, and used as the Coronation Ode of 1902, words by A C Benson.
> Land of Hope and Glory, Mother of the Free,
> How shall we extol thee who are born to thee?
> Wider still and wider shall thy bounds be set;
> God who made thee mighty, make thee mightier yet.

Fox intends the full reference here because its grandiose expression of the then ever growing aspiration for empire and the Kiplingesque, the Churchillian ideal of empire, sadly has become nothing more than an embarrassing irony. Yet, Elgar's lovely music can be involved with a gentler, less grandiloquent theme, more in keeping with the tender nature of the march. Perhaps, different words can create a truer synthesis of words with music rather as William Blake's 1804 "Jerusalem" was rendered by Charles Parry in 1916 for the women's "Fight for the Right" to vote movement, and adjusted by Elgar in 1922 into the beautiful anthem we now know on the terraces. Thus, Fox's 41st and last song for the planned 2003 edition of his "Songs of Nocence" is a new and re-vitalised version of "Land of Hope and Glory" still set to Elgar's march number one.

suds[144] of the marketing era. Behind the stories of our times lies the soapmaker cleaning up through the manufacture of a mass reality of consumptive needs debilitating minds now awash with Bernaysian[145] desires. Here, with all this in mind, lies the power behind modern suborning and manipulating, that has become less a strategy of domination than the resurrection of the feudal, the mere instinct to power. Thus, the chroniclers are mere corporate mouthpieces working the streets and studios of simple minds with scripts that bring them to the final sting[146], that final trick of the public tear conniving with the consumption of loss as if it were grief. Grief is the price of love[147], and of love only; not another product to embellish teeshirts, not actors weeping.

Now the pressure, the squeeze on established public reserve, of feelings properly assumed though undisplayed, the sticking to form and process, the stiff upper lip, are all sloshed aside. No more leaving the

---

[144] 'Suds', Chambers gives, from 1548, *suddes* 'dregs, leavings, muck', a 'marsh' or 'bog'; Ayto is firmer in suggesting not only Middle Dutch *sudse*, 'marsh', but 'boil' from Middle German *suth*, and thence *seethe*, to 'boil'.

[145] Edward L Bernays, 1891-1994, father of Public Relations, nephew of Sigmund Freud, 1856-1939. Bernays led the conversion of corporate and state America to exploit the Freudian management of socio-economic growth through the expansion of consumer demand by the manipulation of unconscious human desires to create popular (mass) needs. Bernays is, perhaps, one of the most under-rated hidden influences on 20th century society.

[146] The pun on "sting" is to emphasise the stretch between the trick of the soap seller and the way soap actually stings your eyes and the way an audience (the public) can be manipulated (ie American slang 'sting') by displays of emotion. *Sting* OE 'pierce with something sharp'.

[147] This phrase was used by Queen Elizabeth II in her message of condolence to the American people after the September 11th mass murders.

imagination to construe the feelings behind the personæ of position. All is "swamped" by the "froths and foams" of the 20th Century's troublesome sea of change, while 'crap'[148] and 'rap' rhyme and reign with scrap; yet it can all be washed away with soap behind screens of sentimental song[149].

Stanza 5

Fox introduces the Queen's wounds that are themselves the wounds in common with the land and the people. Her wounds are the same wounds that tear the country: the bereavements, the agonies of broken marriages, of lost children, the insidious threats, the rumours and attacks, of helplessness, of abandonment, of anomie among all the threat and array of superfluous goods and provisions, the loss of love and neighbourliness, the confusion, and the crisis of identity from the loss of all natural notion of individual purpose and worth. Here meaning is found only in consumption, it is now the human condition at large. That vast bloody sea of troubles washing at the feet of the pious, who daily dip their rags in the blood and lap up the hurt. Still the pious rule, the ever present parasites still groom the people, train them to take

---

[148] Crap, a word with some medieval origin according to Chambers, but no 'crap' in Ayto or Skeat. Fox says 'crap' comes from one Thomas Crapper the Victorian inventor of an excellent and popular water closet. 'Crap' is thus a Victorian concept.

[149] This refers ironically to the lovely song "Smoke Gets in Your Eyes", lyric by Otto Haurbach and music by Jerome Kern, 1933, from the show "Roberta", starring Fred Astaire and Ginger Rogers with Randolph Scott. The nature of the message of this song is of peculiar relevance to the stoic and undemonstrative character of Elizabeth II who would certainly prefer any tears to have been caused not by a release of public emotion, as it were, but excused as caused by the screen of smoke getting in the eyes.

solace in the blood of others, still commission cauldrons of cruelty to collect and keep the ostentation of sacrifice in their corporate cupboards.

With the punning ambiguity of "those salty smears"[150], and the all too human "solace" taken in the pain of others, Fox leads us back into the lost world of the forest where he and we first saw his face in the poem. Fox shows the earth as a wound alive with past sacrifice. Though Christianity (stanza 6) has overgrown the shallow graves of this past, the dead therein still inhabit the earth to satisfy the needs of the living. Again, with the intense use of etymology, puns and reference, Fox unearths the druidic, the primitive practices of our forebears: the human sacrifice, the cannabalistic nature of such bloody sacrifice at the dark heart of our deep pagan past, carried yet to this very day in the Christian Eucharist in which the Christ's flesh is eaten and his blood is supped over and over again. Yes, the endless, invigorating consumption of Christ, the King.

The stanza delves the killing ground we hold in common, wherein lies the "hidden bane'[151]. Fox digs up, exposes the history of the constitutional monarchy, the "splits in stem and stock", back through the Civil War and through its Shakespearean phase, and back down into the very roots of the Island of Britain[152] and

---

[150] 'Smears', this pun draws out the literal smearing of the face with tears, a meaning confirmed by its homophonic nearness, while it takes on the meaning of smearing someone's 'good' name with gossip or lies; while, of course, the salty taste is that of blood.

[151] The hidden 'bane'; Chambers and Skeat give, 'cause of harm, murder, death, wound'.

[152] The appalling spectre always remains of the raw opening of new and old divides in a country much riven throughout its past until the present day by inter-tribal struggles for domination. William Chaney is quite definite in his "The

into the ancient abyss[153]. Here heads are once again trophies of victory, not merely tropes of a poet whose

---

Cult of Kingship in Anglo-Saxon England, MUP, 1970, pages 118-19 that:
> Oswald's decapitation has parallels in 'head-hunting in the north, witnessed in England by the carrying away of the heads of Edwin of Northumbria and Earl Byrhtnoth after their deaths in battle. Oswald's divided body, like that of the Scandinavian Halfdan the Black and Edwin of Northumbria, may have been a ritual interment to provide good seasons in different sections of the realm he had ruled so notably. Indeed the very water in which his bones were washed gave the earth on which it was poured *gratiae salutaris ... effectum [the effect of wholesome benefits]*.

The practice of half hanging then drawing the living guts and quartering the living torso continued well into Elizabethan times.

[153] Though much quoted, Cæsar's 52BC report of customs and behaviours of the Gallic tribes surely applied to pre-Christian Britain in regard to human sacrifice, "The Conquest of Gaul", Cæsar, translated S A Blandford, Penguin, 1951, page 33:
> As a nation the Gauls are extremely superstitious; and so persons suffering from serious diseases, as well as those who are exposed to the perils of battle, offer, or vow to offer, human sacrifices, for the performance of which they employ Druids. They believe that the only way of saving a man's life is to propitiate the god's wrath by rendering another life in its place, and they have colossal images made of wickerwork, the limbs of which they fill with living men; they are then set on fire and burnt to death. They think that the gods prefer the execution of men taken in the act of theft or brigandage, or guilty of some offence; but when they run short of criminals, they do not hesitate to make up with innocent men.

This suggests a Cæsar detached from superstition and little savouring the sacrifice of humans to propitiate gods, let alone for the mere diversion of the Roman mobs. Cæsar was murdered before having to witness the onset of such degeneration of the Roman Empire.

head rests in the laurels of the past, but heads wrested[154] from sacral persons, lifted and hung upon trees.

Stanza 6

The shift in the demonstrative from "there" in stanza one, to "here", and the return to the first person plural ("we"), finds Fox in the forest directly involved,

---

[154] The pun "wrested", rested, apart from its intrinsic value, has the lovely effect of referring to those beautiful lines charting the deepest and painfullest of all British historical ambiguities in the regard of Oliver Cromwell and the beheading of King Charles I. The lines are from Andrew Marvel's "An Horatian Ode Upon Cromwell's Return From Ireland", 1650, lines 55-64,

> While round the armèd bands
> Did clap their bloody hands
> *He* nothing common did or mean
> Upon that memorable scene:
> But with his keener eye
> The axe's edge did try:
> Nor called the gods with vulgar spite
> To vindicate his helpless right,
> But bowed his comely head,
> Down, as upon a bed.

Marvel's exceptional use of puns, "Down", "bowed", "try", "vindicate"[1647], "common", powerfully expresses the appalling, yet inevitable, ambivalence toward Cromwell and the Crown, to the taking of the King's Head, to the spilling of 'divine' blood amongst the commons, to be soaked in their rags. It is a pity such a fine poetic is confined in such a narrow prosodic cage, when it should fly free and high above the mere mortals who comprise its subject. The ode as a whole seems confined by its form, though apt for the lines quoted here. Such a pity the long dead Horace, the true and natural master of this eponymous form, should have been raised by Marvel to contain the expression of his own thought on the complex subject of Cromwell and that clean different thing King Charles I. Perhaps, Horace's own 'royal' constraints may be of some relevance in this regard. Fox, is sensitive to the irony that this remark should feature here in a footnote to his "Fairy Queen", of all poems.

no longer observing, but again an actor among others in the scene itself.

This stanza brings the sacrilege of the mistletoe[155] into conjunction with the new age of Christian conversion. Fox's use of internal as well as end rhyme quickens the life of the past and brings back the ancient ways. The old ways have not died, but lie in wait to burst upon the present, to come from time past to time present, ambiguously "from time to time", ensuring they are perhaps always present in time future.

The introduction of groves and graves[156] takes us into the depths of the past. The use of "grow" and "burst" and the bbb marriage in the rhyme of mistletoe, know(ledge) and (blood) flow, lead to the roots of crime[157], the secretion[158] of life's blood in all our hearts. Above all it is Fox's reference to Diana the huntress,

---

[155] Mistletoe, Ayto not helpful, but Skeat finds that OE (AS) *misteltán* and through to the idea of bird lime in (oak) trees where deposits of ingested seeds allow promulgation of the mistletoe plant. Skeat says mistletoe is literally 'birdlime twig'.

[156] The root of 'grave' is a thing cut, engraved and hence the burial pit, the furrow as Fox puts it, of the seeds so long lain buried in the 'groves' which Skeat indicates has etymological synonymity with 'grave' through OE *gráf*. The seeds of our primitive past are not dead, but lie in the depths of us, always threatening to burst forth among us.

[157] The use of "crime" at this point finds the ambiguity of the early meaning 'to decide' and the evolution of such decision to the subject itself, the act itself that is being judged. Ayto shows a relationship with 'certain', 'critic', 'decree', 'discriminate', 'excrement', 'secret'.

[158] As above, "secret", according to Ayto, Chambers, Skeat, etymologically is L *secretus* 'separated' and *sē* "apart" and *cernere* 'separate', hence taking us back to the removal of hearts in sacrifice; but also to 'secretion' (of fluids) along another division of the root. Skeat gives, through 'concern', the Sanskrit *sri* to pour (cut) out, through Aryan root SKAR to 'cut shear cleave'.

whose seizure at the heart of the crown created confusion and left the people in a profusion of tears. The etymological punning of 'hunt'[159] with to seize and seize with seizure of the heart and the pun 'hart'[160] all refer to Diana's bloody trail through the forest hunting out the hearts of the people while causing seizures throughout the 'Palace'. Fox leaves the reader with endless scope to find Diana as both perpetrator and victim, as paradoxically the hunter and the hunted. This is double edged poetry of great justice, a poetry that leaves our hearts unresolved, still haunted by the hunting of Diana.

Such heartsblood flows into the next stanza where our eyes drink in the scene literally of the Queen as she processed through Bath and the ancient scene conjured by Fox from the roots of the forest as we are moved to cheer and our tongues unfold again the old stories even here today among the wooden hearts of a modern people. This leaves the question to hang as to why on earth we stayed so long freezing in the cold just to see her pass in a few seconds from our sight?

Stanza 7

The poem itself was completed by May 21st 2002 and finally revised 25th May, prior to the four days of the main Jubilee celebration in London 31st May through 4th June 2002, centred on Buckingham

---

[159] Ayto gives "hunt" as from OE *hentan* 'seize', but it is an ancient word going back to Indo-European *kend-* while Skeat goes to the Aryan root *KAR* 'fall'.

[160] This pun is a direct reference the Princess Diana, the huntress, whose quarry was the horned beast, her cuckolded husband, Charles. Chambers gives 'hart' as a 'male deer', developed from OE *heorot, heort* AD725 Beowulf, and variously by several paths to 'horned animal', also Skeat, but not referenced by Ayto.

Palace. Fox realised that Brian May's [161] National Anthem was doomed to thunder from the top of the palace, at the Queen's pleasure, echoing, with perhaps a little less satirical bite than the original "God Save The Queen" on the 1975 Album. Doubtless the ironic glee of it had Freddie Mercury, the original 'fairy queen' of the pop world, very much in mind. Nevertheless, it was certainly game set and match for the 'real' Queen, surrounded by kneeling, newly appointed popular knights waiting to rise to the lightest touch of her sword upon their fashionable collars.

---

[161] Lead guitarist of the Queen, a popular British rock group originating in the 1970s whose lead vocalist, the volatile if poisonous Freddie Mercury, was the ultimate 'queen' boldly committed to outrage and 'aggro' (aggression). In the slang of that time, and still now, 'queen' meant homosexual, as did 'fairy' and as, more recently, 'gay'. Freddie died in London in 1991 of an AIDS related disease. They released their most famous album through EMI in 1975 "A Night At The Opera", with Freddie Mercury lead singer, Brian May writer and lead guitar, Roger Taylor percussion, John Deacon electric bass. Queen are probably one of the few late 20th century groups to create work that deserves some sort of lasting interest, outside the inevitable e-shrines of adoring, if uncritical gays. Nevertheless, any close examination of their lyrics reveals disappointing missed opportunities, but this would seem to quibble with mere detail when comparing Queen to the usual drivel that dominates the iconic pop world. The album includes the ever popular "Bohemian Rhapsody", the last song on the album, which then concludes, satirically, with the national anthem "God Save The Queen" in imitation of the curtain at a real night at the opera. Ironically, the last laugh is now with the 'real' Queen, 2002; although the 'unreal' queen Freddie, "The Faerie Kinge", would no doubt have smiled ruefully at the spectacle of Brian May playing the specially arranged anthem at full blast from the roof of Buckingham Palace. Doubtless, the extraordinary Mercury would have adored the whole thing as it was so, so over the top, so ... bizarre.

Thus, Fox encapsulates the splendid tension between the times, as it were, when the seemingly straitlaced Windsors slip through a vast soap screen to pop from their own bubble of history into the bigger global world where they are able to shine once more as if raised from the rainbow's end. Such organisation, such military precision, such a famous victory.

Looking back into the stanza "our eyes drink in" the scene of the "secret crime", but it is our lips and tongues that "unfold", that are released to find the enchanted Queen, the Faerie Queene, with us here and now. The stanza draws us through its ramified ambiguities to envisage the reality where our wooden hearts are in fact those hearts of oak of the ancient forests that became the oaks sacrificed to build the navy of Henry VIII that became the navy of Nelson. The oak now stands for the courage that lifted the British from the merely tribal to the merely triumphant. Yet, beneath the foliage of triumphalism lies ensconced an era of extraordinary invention, new vision and moral evolution. Fox unravels the weave, the fabric of the present until we can just pick up the threads that lead us into to the nature of the forest we are actually in. Here we have waited, overwhelmed by the frozen catastrophe of a bare and leafless winter, a disaster ridden 20th century, while fearful, sunless days adumbrate a future starved of light when the goodness of the sunlit plains of recent times could pass, could be lost so easily forever.

The dull Autumn sun must bow to the nether gods, must lour in winter's bare, cold, darkness. The spell is bleak and dangerous calling for sacrifice. There is nothing until the cries of the forest of people raise the head of the monarch of the sky and she rises again "her head all bowed[162] with gold", just as the sun at last

---

[162] The pun on "bowed" (boughed) calls up the ancient rites of Fraser's Golden Bough. This is to risk the "bow wow" gibe

rises after the winter months, so she rises, and comes into our vision. We are taken directly back to Spenser[163] through Fox's use of "glistered"[164], and on through Spenser's "Faerie Queene" to his roots in the

---

once current when 'everything' seemed explicable by reference to Fraser and Jessie Weston. Such a gibe would obscure the branch meaning derived from the structural tension caused by the opposition between 'bowed' down and rising from the lower, the nether position.

[163] The word glistered is from "The Faerie Queene", Book I, Canto IV, Stanza 8:

> High above all a cloth of state was spred,
> And a rich throne, as bright as sunny day;
> On which there sate, most brave embellished
> With royall robes and gorgeous array,
> A mayden queene that shone, as Titans ray,
> In glistring gold and perelesse pretious stone;
> Yet her bright blazing beautie did assay
> To dim the brightness of her glorious throne,
> As envying her selfe, that too exceeding shone:

This is the Canto on the "... sinfull hous of Pryde...", reference to which reinforces the ambivalence of Fox's "bowed", "weighed down with gold" and the "broken" god Vallhalla whose populous sky is broken, re-made as 'Yahweh' and, in turn, reborn as Christ the sole occupant, who, although a trinity, is not tritheistic, but a form of pure monodomination. Of course, the proverbial "all that glisters is not gold, often have you heard that told" has a long tradition in English, back through Gray, Shakespeare, and Chaucer, and perhaps to earliest times. Here it completes the stanza both with its ambivalent tradition and with the image of a sun struggling once more to break through a long winter.

[164] As already mentioned in the introduction, "glistered" is an obsolete form of 'glittered'. Fox has introduced this form for reasons it is unnecessary to enumerate in detail, nevertheless amongst other effects the sound and form generate an effect similar to the fortuitous "mistaking", the bumping into the "unbeknownst", that Christopher Ricks, op cit, essayed from the "beresk" wordsmitherie of a Bristol (UK) constable in the 1980s.

ancient forests and a sky once more divided between competing gods.

Stanza 8

Here we find a people with hope. The stanza sings, rejoices, is alive with the warmth and power of the rising sun. The stanza stretches and wakes and faces the "blinding" brightness of the sun's "goodness" as it falls through the canopy and down to us amongst the tangled roots of the forest floor. Here the Foxian ambiguities riddle our feelings as we try to look up to the sun, to the source of light, of vision. Yet we are forced to avert our gaze, forced to look down to see the effect of such power upon the earth to which we are ineluctably bound. Energy is tensed like potential lightning drawn from the clashing images of "blindness", of "casting" down[165], of "brilliance" as a

---

[165] This is an allusion to Fox's 1967 poem "Transitory Good Warmth", volume 3, "Insistence":

> Transitory good warmth, flurry of sun in the valley
> And in valleys below that.
>
> I, the watcher
> In this feeling of warmth,
> Am embraced by movements of light
> And carried a silver haired child,
> To the small stream down below;
> But below the valley in the still pools
> Is the core of the earth,
> Where Sunheart pumps red sunsets over a land,
> A land where I have a world
> Which I may have been the centre of
>
> Or on a spiral point
>   Where
> Ghost and white bone flake
> Touch snow and glisten into one another
> Of the future where I shall go
> And be burned by cold flames

slightly suspect word, of an "eye" of light that watches "tangled in the past", all within the double indemnity of "down".

The lightning flashes light the scene and we find ourselves brought indoors beneath a mere canopy, a domestic furnishing of gnat like significance, a fine lace net. The use of 'canopy'[166] of lace, of netting, domesticates the ancient, primitive forest, draws us back into the crowded street into the built environment of the herenow, the occasion of the Fairy Queen's visit to Bath. Though punning as the forest canopy, beneath which we are merely part of a crowd, Fox is returned to his position in stanza one, and we are carried with him.

The compression, the mixing of feelings brings us to the joyfully expansive last lines of the stanza which lead us beautifully back, with our eyes lowered, to find a way through knowledge of the "ancient lore"[167] back into the "winding", the "endless wood" of the last stanza. The flash of images, the clash of the old and the new, and the tension between the nature of the

---

And see half statements of fire
dieing away.

[166] Ayto gives 'canopy' as 'a mosquito net', from Greek *kōnōpeion* derived through *kōnops* 'mosquito', and, for good effect, through to the slightly ridiculous *canapé*, which seems somewhat appropriate (to Fox).

[167] We have yet another example of Fox's use of etymology to hone the poetry of this stanza. Ayto, as Chambers and Skeat, gives 'lore' as OE *lār* 'learn', but Ayto tracks down prehistoric West Germanic **liznōjan*, which also produced German *lernen*. This goes back ultimately to an indo-European **leis-* 'track', and so seems to carry the underlying notion of 'gaining experience by following a track'. Ayto does declare that * indicates that the word itself cannot be found as such, but that it is reasonable on the circumstantial evidence available for it to be postulated. However, from Fox's point of view, Ayto takes the word back to its roots among the forest tracks and paths of old when to know your way was indeed a matter of life or death.

crown and the nature of the metaphor that carries it creates the energy that drives the verse from its highest position in the firmament to its lowest intrusion of radiance into the depths of the forest floor. Here it gives up life to the huddle and muddle of humankind crying out to see the light, desperate for the golden vision of a real god, here among them, open to the touch.

Stanza 9

The image here is again dependent on the literal reference to Fox among the "forest of faces" in the opening stanza. Here, in the final stanza, we find ourselves still in "the endless" forest winding along the "well worn way" looking down, seeing and following our tangled roots in the earth beneath our feet where the fallen good lies gathered, a good which is, literally, the golden warmth of the sun, cast down in the previous stanza. We are returned to our roots in the common clay, wherein humankind was moulded and from which, with Nietzchean vision, we may try to rise above ourselves and break free of our earthly roots. But, we find that we are even yet, paradoxically, held fast, stuck in the clay by an ineradicable need to bask and bake our day in the golden light of the sun, whereof new life shoots forth and the forests are renewed.

Fox beautifully expresses that, however we, humankind, may try casting off the light of the sun, somehow it is to cast off the ancient protector, the unknowable lifesource whose loss can only mean darkness and death. We are left in the forest knowing that all renewal, all new growth certainly depends on the sun, and that the sun must somehow figure in our ordinary[168] daily lives, and that the behaviour of an

---

[168] Ayto gives 'ordinary' as from L. *ōrdinārius* 'following the usual course [path]'.

human sun in social figuration of our lives must be good, cannot be otherwise or less. /

Yet, the stanza seems to hold that rising above the life-giving source seems too high an aspiration when our feet are held fast to the old ways. We are not free to fly from the forest in spite of all the appearance of modernity, of the postmodern and now the cybennial converting its mysteries to havens of blinding explanation. The layering leafmould that forms and renews the forest floor is broken through by new shoots which seem to break the mould and find the light. In this we are left to consider the nature of such 'renewal'. Though new, are the "growing shoots" different or merely cyclic? Indeed, what is that 'vision" holding them fast?

So much seems to depend on the cyclical sacrifice to this ideal, on the inexplicable need endlessly to set up then tear down, and again and again to resurrect a god on earth, that idol of our hearts to be raised by the people, adored and destroyed in turn. Now matter how well lit and interconnected our caves have virtually become, still we sit hunched behind our own thoughts driving them out, beyond the selves of us, here, eyes gleaming in the dark, dreaming.

Conclusion

It can be seen from the serendipitous nature of the above that neither Fox nor I operate with a large scale hypothesis in mind wherein all this stuff fits. Fox has ended up a poet, he says, because of poor memory, and lack of scholastic ability which leaves him at the mercy of constant re-invention. In consequence, it seems to me, that through his over-dependence on poetic intelligence he has ended up closer to the anarchy of 'reality' than those whose thoughts are organised to make sense. 'Sense' is necessarily perspectival, perhaps determined by a convenient preconception, a grand scheme, a view of things that is merely a convenient disposing of the human psyche toward efficient comfort. 'Sense' is thus always prescriptive, and too much sense prescribes the poetic, fencing the open range where the poet should roam free.

That I should, as Fox's editor, generate all these 'other' words to do with "The Fairy Queen" enlivens the paradox that some poetry, and certainly Fox's, packs enormous energy of meaning in a seemingly simple nucleus of form and words. Unleashing the energy contained in such a nucleus is somewhat risky, the fallout being potentially fatal to normality. Yet, "The Fairy Queen" does what Fox's poetry does best: it efficiently encapsulates a tortuous 'plexus' of meaning about its subject in a deceptively recognisable form, in few words, simply. It illustrates, too, Fox's crucial and all pervading perspective: that meaning *is* feeling.

If you've got this far, friend, then you'll have worked out that we are, in the end, just two characters in search of an audience; and if you have been it, thanks.